PRAISE FOR LONG LIVE LOVE

Long Live Love is a triumphant story about escaping generational trauma through the freedom Jesus offers us. By sharing the honesty of her struggle out of her toxic family system, Rena Roberts demonstrates the courage and wisdom it takes to confront her past, rewrite her story, and find new patterns of relationship that will serve her well in the future. She is both a skilled therapist and a trauma overcomer, and her vulnerability and wisdom combine to encourage and enlighten you. This book is a valuable tool to help people break the cycle of dysfunction in their past and set a new course for generations to come.

> — WAYNE JACOBSEN,
> Host of The God Journey
> Author of *He Loves Me* and co-author of *The Shack*

I had the great pleasure of working with Rena Roberts for several years at my treatment center for eating disorders. She is an insightful and accomplished clinician and, as I told her in the past, a great writer with lots of important, intense, difficult, and transformational things to say. Rena has shown up with this and more in *Long Live Love*. In this book, Rena takes readers on a journey through her past as she embraces God to help her heal old wounds and break free, all while prompting readers to go on the quest with her to heal from their own. After finishing the book, I found myself once again talking to and giving to homeless people, something I had not done for quite some time. Readers looking for a deeply personal and spiritual book that beckons them to learn how to love and forgive all through connection with Holy Spirit can turn to *Long Live Love* for just that.

> — CAROLYN COSTIN
> The Carolyn Costin Institute
> Author of *8 Keys to Recovery From an Eating Disorder*

The Creator intends to set humanity free from oppression (Luke 4:18–19). *Long Live Love* takes an unflinching look at this promise in the context of generational trauma. With wisdom born of training and experience, Rena Roberts recounts the compelling story of how God used community, therapy, and disappointment to set her free from dysfunctional familial patterns. This honest and courageous spiritual memoir will inspire readers to embrace fully God's promises of freedom, forgiveness, and spiritual intimacy.

— KINDALEE PFREMMER DE LONG, PhD, MA

Pepperdine University
Associate Dean of Seaver College
Blanche E. Seaver Professor of Religion

———

Long Live Love is a must-read for those looking to genuinely walk in the newness of life that Christ promises to the redeemed. Written with an inviting vulnerability of the personal work of the Spirit of God in her own life, Rena Roberts candidly shares the simple, yet often overlooked, key to experiencing joy in the midst of suffering, life in the midst of loss, and freedom in the midst of fear. I would recommend this book to any and all who desire to see *forgiveness* lived out as the ever-resounding legacy of Christian faith and liberty in a culture that so desperately needs what only Christ can give.

— PASTOR JOSH EPSTEIN

Castle Rock Community Church, CO

———

In *Long Live Love,* Rena Roberts displays her full vulnerability, strength, and wisdom as she takes us on her healing journey and her ever-deepening relationship with God to release from bondage and find greater personal freedom and peace. She gently and skillfully invites us to examine our own lives and how we, too, might live and act with less fear and more love, something the world desperately needs more of right now.

— JESSICA NAGLER LOWENSTEIN, M.A., LMFT

Psychotherapist, spiritual teacher, and award-winning author of *Jun Q'anil: One Who Walks the Way*

Rena is one of the most genuine people I know. Her vulnerability is refreshing! She demonstrates, with beauty and grace, the depth of the riches of following the wisdom and knowledge of God, even when you don't understand His ways. For someone who desires to learn how to gain freedom through a relationship with Jesus, this book will provoke deep soul-searching exercises that will help you draw closer to the heart of Abba.

— PASTOR BARBARA HUSTON

Daughter of the King
Kingdom Streams Church

This candid, personal testimony of Rena's journey in life is very interesting and open. Surrendering to Christ and His Word as Lord of our lives is where true freedom can be found. Rena and Jeff's family life show this journey through the challenges they have overcome by the Power of God's grace and the help of the Holy Spirit. May it be an encouragement to all on that Journey.

— PASTOR JIM DIXON

Church of Shaver Lake, CA

Be prepared to embark on a deeply personal journey with Rena Roberts from bondage to freedom. *Long Live Love* shares her gripping story in an intensely personal way with refreshing transparency. Rena explores a theological understanding of her transformation, simultaneously sharing her real life, real grit, real suffering, and real freedom. She delicately yet directly challenged me to wrestle with my own hidden fears and generational issues, describing a freedom I have longed for and discarded as unattainable long ago. Rena has given me the amazing gift of hope and the biblical tools to choose freedom instead of fear. If you have lost hope, believe it can be rekindled. Approach this book with an open heart, and though the journey will not be an easy one, there is true, real-life freedom to be experienced.

— PAUL MEITLER

World Impact Missionary
Camp Director (2010-2020)
Oaks Camp & Conference Center

Long Live Love

Walking Out Freedom From Painful Generational Patterns

RENA ROBERTS

Long Live Love: Walking Out Freedom from Painful Generational Patterns

Copyright © 2023 by Rena Roberts. Published by Long Live Love Publishing. All rights reserved.

For more information about this book and the author, please contact by email rena@renaroberts.com, or visit www.renaroberts.com.

Editing/Production by Jennifer Edwards Communications, jedwardsediting.net
Cover Design and Interior Layout & Typography by Linné Garrett, 829design.com
Cover Art by Sophia Beccue
Author Photographs by Lisa Lorene Photography

Paperback: 979-8-9879969-0-4

Hardcover: 979-8-9879969-1-1

E-book: 979-8-9879969-2-8

Audiobook: 979-8-9879969-3-5

Library of Congress Control Number: 2023904809

Unless otherwise indicated, all Scripture quotations are taken from THE HOLY BIBLE, NEW IN-TERNATIONAL VERSION®, NIV® Copyright © 1973, 1978, 1984, 2011 by Biblica, Inc.® Used by permission. All rights reserved worldwide.

Scriptures marked NLT come from *Holy Bible*, New Living Translation, copyright © 1996, 2004, 2015 by Tyndale House Foundation. Used by permission of Tyndale House Publishers, Inc., Carol Stream, Illinois 60188. All rights reserved.

Scriptures marked ESV come from The ESV® Bible (The Holy Bible, English Standard Version®). ESV® Text Edition: 2016. Copyright © 2001 by Crossway, a publishing ministry of Good News Publishers. The ESV® text has been reproduced in cooperation with and by permission of Good News Publishers. Unauthorized reproduction of this publication is prohibited. All rights reserved.

Scripture quotations marked MSG are taken from *THE MESSAGE*, copyright © 1993, 2002, 2018 by Eugene H. Peterson. Used by permission of NavPress. All rights reserved. Represented by Tyndale House Publishers, Inc.

Scripture quotations marked NKJV are taken from the New King James Version®. Copyright © 1982 by Thomas Nelson. Used by permission. All rights reserved.

Disclaimer: This book reflects the author's present recollections of her own experiences over time. Some names and characteristics have been changed to protect their confidentiality, some events have been compressed, and some dialogue has been recreated.

DEDICATION

I dedicate this book to my grandchildren,
the Lewis boys—Franklin, Henry (Hank), and Levi,
who inspire me to bring generational freedom,
which manifests as God's supernatural Love
everywhere to everyone, especially them.

I love you, precious grandsons.

"From the beginning, I have set you apart to be
a forerunner for breaking family chains.

I gave you wisdom and discernment as a child.

Do not work only in the flesh, which is control and fear,

But total freedom comes through the Spirit."

These words came to my spirit while praying about writing this book. I believe my destiny is to break generational curses and restore my family line back to God's destiny of blessing. When the Lord spoke to Jeremiah, He said, "Before I formed you in the womb I knew you, before you were born I set you apart; I appointed you as a prophet to the nations" (Jeremiah 1:5 NIV). This verse confirms that I have been appointed, set apart, for something specific. During a personal crisis, these words took on a deeper, more real meaning to me when I began to experience true freedom from painful generational patterns that were holding me back. I understood my purpose was first to break free and then show others how to do the same. I know this because freedom from generational bondage is written on my heart, and I've had so much opposition to it in my life.

CONTENTS

FOREWORD

A week before Covid-19 put the world on lockdown, Rena Roberts came into my world. I sought her out after hearing how she experienced a transformed life. What really struck me was her radical humility, her incredible vulnerability, and her thankful declaration of the freedom she walks in now.

When I approached Rena, I was serving many people in a local church, in charge of a very large Bible Study, and mentoring many, yet privately, I was suffering. I've always loved Jesus and His people, but due to experiencing some tremendous losses in my life, I was like an emotional live wire, and I didn't even know what to ask for. I saw and sensed a freedom in Rena that I'd been searching for my entire life.

Rena is an incredible listener and friend, providing refuge in the storm for me. As she walked me through the process that had given her a new life, she was like Jesus to me, helping me see my struggles for what they were—struggles to take to Jesus for repair and healing. Not a referendum on who I was as a person. I was struck by the focus Rena kept as the goal of our time together—FREEDOM!

The first thing she told me in our time together was to go low and go slow—humble yourself and slow down everything . . . thoughts, speech, reactions, behaviors. Living "low and slow" became the first way of getting my life back. As Rena and I lived life together, I learned from the way she lived. She really is that person we read about in Scripture who gave me not only the gospel but her very life. I had a front-row seat to watch how she regularly put into practice the things she taught me. Yes, she did exhort me to put relationships over being right, and yes, she did encourage me to drop my resentment and forgive in a radical way. She did ask me to ask the Holy Spirit, "What is my part?" But the crazy part was the way she was showing me the path to transformation through how she lived. She was showing me, not telling me. Not sin sniffing, preaching at me, correcting me, confronting me, or trying to exert control over me. I watched her working out a supernatural way of living in real-time on a daily basis in her own life.

I remember the day I was promoting my view that I believed was right, and someone else was wrong. She calmly and lovingly said to me, "Jesus is the only right One. Let's pray and ask the Holy Spirit what your part is." She shared her personal stories of transformation, moving from resentment, judgment, control, manipulation, pride, and wishing the worst on others to a whole different way of thinking, living, and loving . . . I mean, this girl is the REAL DEAL. Rena is a very special person, and I will never forget the way she walked with me, showing me supernatural love and incredible kindness while she helped me reorganize my entire life.

The process you read of in this book is life-altering, stripping away those layers of denial to really face the objective truth of what you are thinking, feeling, and doing. When you read this book you will see that Rena lays out spiritual guideposts that create a new relationship for engaging with God, self, and others. Rena has laid out an outstanding roadmap for us to unpack so much history, underlying pain, and immaturity. She then gently illuminates the way to rebuild your life in a meaningful and practical, intimate relationship with the Holy Spirit.

I've learned so much through this journey with the Holy Spirit, but the biggest thing I learned from my dear friend and mentor is this—finding spiritual freedom is a life, not a lesson. Thank you for sharing your life with me, Rena.

I'm finally free.

Praise Him.

— LEIGH ANNE TSUJI
Strategist | Project Coach
Founder, Love What You Stand For
leighannetsuji.com

ACKNOWLEDGMENTS

First, Holy Spirit, who inspired and instructed me in writing this book. I can do nothing without Your Spirit living in me.

Barbara Huston, my cousin, dearest friend, and savagely loving pastor. Thank you, Barb, for endeavoring, praying, and pouring hours, days, weeks, and years into teaching, showing, and challenging me to pursue God above all. Thank you for pushing me to die to myself and trust supernaturally. Thank you for showing me how to live out supernatural love.

My husband, Jeff, for believing in me and supporting me throughout our life together. Thank you for supporting this project unconditionally without hesitation. Thank you for believing that I have something to say and wanting to be a part of my work in helping people receive freedom in Christ. I love you.

Leigh Anne Tsuji, my dear friend and inspiring coach. Thank you, Leigh Anne, for showing me that I could make this book happen and guiding me along the way when I felt stuck. You were the perfect kind of support.

Jennifer Edwards, my editor. Thank you, Jennifer, for your easy, confident way. Thank you for catching my vision, honoring my voice, and taking me from the first draft to the final manuscript. I am proud of this project because of your work. You're fantastic!

———

Sophia Beccue, my dear friend and gifted artist. Thank you, Sophia, for creating such a beautiful piece to adorn the cover of my book. You made my dream sequence for this project a reality. All glory to God, who has gifted you and continues to flow His beauty through your heart and hands (and paint brushes). But before that, thank you for knowing, holding, and praying for me through so much pain.

———

Linné Garrett, my graphic designer. Thank you, Linné, for your excitement and encouragement from the beginning. And thank you for bringing luxury to the reader with your lovely book design and typographic talents.

———

Steven Lewis, my son-in-law. Thank you, Steven, for wrecking my life and destroying my dreams so Jesus could get a hold of me. I love you.

———

I must also acknowledge my children, Amanda, Nick, and Joey, for your support and excitement as I have worked on this book. I'm so blessed to have each of you. I especially acknowledge Amanda for her courage to be herself and support me in sharing part of our story.

———

And finally, to so many friends and fans. You know who you are! I love you, and thank you.

INTRODUCTION

Since I was a little girl, I've yearned for a loving, healthy family. My parents are very broken humans whose parents were also broken and chained humans. And so it was, all the way back through the ocean of ancestors who came before me. I thought I would break those chains by being a good parent, and my children's lives would reflect that blessing. But, I'm learning I have no control over people or circumstances, and trying to control them is prideful. Breaking the chains is a spiritual process, and changed behavior must be a manifestation of spiritual cleansing and freedom rather than an exercise of the will. I tried to do it the other way around, and believe me, it did not work.

When I was thirteen and VHS was new technology, my stepdad and I watched the first two Rocky movies at home. That began my love for the character "Rocky." I have seen every Rocky movie. I love them all . . . I guess because Rocky always beats the odds. He chases his dream despite crushing insecurities. I love him because he is self-reflective and admits his faults.

But most importantly, I love how Rocky overcame his family of origin and broke abusive patterns. We don't learn much about Rocky's family of origin, but we know his father spoke curses over him—"You're a bum!"— and physically abused him. We see the severe brokenness in his soul when he breaks down in the first Rocky movie to his trainer, Mickey.

Rocky's success despite dark family baggage is impressive. I think the movies continue to be successful because we want Rocky's courage and strength. And we all want to break free from our families' dictates to become our own men or women, free from pathological mindsets and wounds and behaviors. Who, when asked if they dreamed of becoming an alcoholic like their parents, would say yes? Yet statistics show that children from an alcoholic home are four times more likely to become alcoholics.[1] Who, when asked if they dreamed of creating an abusive home like their parents, would say yes? Yet children from abusive homes are up to seven times more likely to have abuse in their homes as adults.[2] This pattern is consistent with virtually every pathological family pattern.

In real life, victory over destructive generational patterns is rare. Psychologists have studied pathological family patterns for decades, trying to discover why they persist. Why are the sins of the father visited down to the third and fourth generations, as Exodus 20:5 says, even when those descendants do not want to repeat the family patterns?

For me, the opposition to freedom has been strong, shocking, and continuous, which only confirms that the Lord has plans for me to overcome it—to fulfill my destiny of breaking painful generational patterns, restoring my family line to God's destiny, and encouraging others to do the same. This book shares my journey to freedom in three sections—*Longing, Living,* and *Loving.*

I'll first bring you into the heart and experience of me as a little girl, longing for my ideal family amid clear and deep generational curses. This section on Longing includes how I was victimized and then internalized and acted out the same. The Living section details my determination to live a psychologically healthy and spiritually obedient life by immersing myself in my personal psychotherapy and studying psychology while at the same time establishing a traditional Christian lifestyle. But when all of this good and wise and psychologically-sophisticated living blew up in my face, I found myself bleeding on the floor. The Loving section explains how I found the freedom I had always longed for. This process, from longing to loving, has been utterly transformational. I now believe that living a loving life rooted in true Love itself, which is God, is the absolute only way to break free from generational baggage.

You may have little to no spiritual background in your family. Or maybe your spiritual culture is very different from Christianity. In that case, you probably don't think much about Jesus or go to the Bible for guidance. You may even find those things offensive. Whatever your opinions or background, I encourage you to read my story with an open mind as I share how these things ministered to me, culminating in soul-transforming miracles. Seek God as you understand Him (to borrow from Alcoholics Anonymous). You will see how I was clumsy in my attempts to connect with God deeply, yet the effort was all He needed. That's how I know that Holy Spirit will meet you wherever He finds you.

While utterly broken and at the end of myself, I broke free. And you can too. The stories and events in this book are real and raw, and sometimes hardcore. Really, the situation was pretty ordinary, but God did something extraordinary with me through my pain and surrender to Him. This book won't change you if you're looking for a magic pill or a quick fix. You still should read it and consider my journey as you go along on yours. But if you are broken and willing to lay down your ego, you will eat this up.

I hope my story blesses you and emboldens you to go after freedom recklessly.

PART ONE

Longing

CHAPTER 1

The Back Porch

The back porch was my gateway to a backyard filled with fruit trees and my papa's garden. He owned our home and rented it to my mom and stepdad (Daddy) cheap so that we would have a home to live in. Papa planted a garden every year and maintained several fruit trees on that property. My cousin, Chris, who was nine months older than me, sometimes lived with us along with his entire family of five. When our families lived together, the six children shared one bedroom, and his parents slept on the living room floor on a thick piece of foam they rolled out each night.

Chris and I tore through the back porch, hardly noticing it, to play out back. One of our favorite pastimes was climbing from tree to tree as the fruit trees ripened throughout the seasons. We'd bask in the cherry tree branches and fight off the birds with sticks, which were tricky to lug up the tree without breaking them or accidentally catching them on some part of the tree and knocking ourselves off balance. The apricot trees were too thick with branches to climb, so we'd drag whatever stray sawhorse or lawn chair we could find to reach the sweetest fruit. We loved to lounge in the huge golden delicious apple tree in the fall, trying to detect whether or not a worm had already feasted on the apple we were about to chomp. I can still remember the disgusting bitter flavor of a worm-eaten apple, the high-pitched screech of Chris's laughter, and the twinkle in his small blue eyes as he affectionately made fun of me for being tricked by a worm.

Sometimes we would venture into the chicken coop and dare each other to put a finger through the chicken wire. The chickens always tried to peck our fingers, and we almost always got them out on time. But sometimes we didn't. I never liked those chickens. They scared me. But I did feel sad for them when my papa chopped off the head of one and set it down on its feet to show us how a chicken will run around with its head cut off . . . blood spurting out of its neck. Papa had a sick sense of humor sometimes.

Chris and I learned about nature because we were part of nature. We talked and dreamed and declared how we wanted to live our lives. We had big ideas, ethics, reason, and common sense, and we believed in each other. Without those days and hours together, I'm not sure I would have made it this far.

Sometimes, I'd go to the back porch alone. Mom would order me to go out back and play, but instead, I'd crouch down on the cold and dirty concrete to listen. I was just a little girl on my porch. It was small, only about five feet by twelve feet at the most. There was some sort of half wall, and then the upper half was screened in. One side was blocked by one of the two refrigerators on the porch. The air was stagnant, and the odors would rest there. The smell of dampness, dust, and cat food filled my nose and lungs, along with an occasional waft of the long-stem red rose bush that my papa had planted just outside the spring-loaded screen door that had taken a fingernail from me once.

I'd watch as ants crawled around and on Quinten's cat food. Quinten was the alpha cat of the neighborhood. He was huge and aloof. He had long white fur with large grey patches on his back, shoulders, and tail. His eyes were green, and he had a sweet pink nose surrounded by grey fur. I would often hear the "maaawhing" of cats mating or fighting many summer nights. I was never sure which, and maybe they go together, but they sounded scary. Anyway, Quinten would return the next day with some mortal-looking wound from which he eventually recovered and hop up onto the shelf where his bag of food was kept to tell us he was hungry. I couldn't reach the shelf at the time of my alone episodes on the porch.

Sometimes, I opened one of the refrigerators in childish fidgeting, and the mildewy smell of an old refrigerator filled with aluminum beer cans would mix with the porch smells. Strange how aromas stay with us, how we can close our eyes and remember them years later. I tried to open and close the refrigerator gently because it tended to make a clanking sound, and I didn't want my mother to know I was there, listening from the back porch.

I knew very early that my family was unwell.

I remember one time in particular when my mother was raging! She was berating my daddy, barking profanity at him and shaming him, calling him a drunk, weak, and stupid. She threatened to divorce him, and things were getting violent. I heard things hitting the walls as she tore into closets pulling out suitcases or something, saying she was taking me and my brother, Jim, with her. At first, my daddy tried to de-escalate the situation by making an affectionate joke in response to her f-words. He said, "C'mon, Linda, don't act nuts." Finally, when he'd had enough, he barked ugly profane words back, daring her to go ahead and leave if that's what she wanted. It became an ugly pattern.

At those times, my fear and grief became unbearable. I'm sure I dissociated because I have no memory of what happened next. I probably went to my imagination for solace. But we never did leave.

Other times, I would hear my mother's sobs and hysterical grief. She'd threaten suicide, saying she couldn't take it anymore. She'd shriek that she hated her life, she hated her body, she hated having to take care of everyone. She'd make Daddy promise to take care of Jimmy and me. Through her pathetic tears, she'd order him to tell me she loved me so much and that she was sorry. I wanted to run in and beg her not to kill herself, and I think I did that once. But she was so hysterical that it terrified me. I froze. I knew my pleas would only fill her with more guilt and grief, so I curled up in a ball on the porch and listened and hoped and prayed that my mommy would be happy and okay.

Longing for a Healthy Family

I can't remember not wanting a different kind of family. I loved my family. There were good things about us, but I knew very early that my family was unwell. I wanted a family where people resolved conflict and grew from their mistakes. I wanted a family where people thrived and became better because family surrounded them. Most kids seem to accept their family until they are old enough to analyze and question standards. But I can't ever remember a time when I thought my family's shenanigans were okay.

I think I was different, in part, because of the age of television in which I emerged. It may sound funny, but I'm sure this contributed to my awareness. My favorite shows were *Leave It to Beaver* (re-runs, I'm not that old) and *The Brady Bunch*. When most little girls my age wanted to be Cinderella or Snow White, I fantasized about having a family like the Cleavers or the Bradys. I dreamed of having an intact family where the dad worked hard all day and came home to a calm and reassuring wife who had the dinner table set where the entire family sat down together to eat. Whatever conflicts or crises these families faced, they acted responsibly or respectfully toward each other, apologized, and turned earnestly from their bad behavior. They weren't perfect, but they admitted and grew from their mistakes. And their problems were not outside of the normal scope of problems. There weren't alcoholics, drug addicts, pedophiles, and people in federal prison within their immediate or extended family.

Okay, so obviously, I was as idealistic as my friends who wanted to be Cinderella or even one of Charlie's angels, for that matter. None of those fantasies are based on reality. Still, I knew the habits and lifestyles of my family were far from the realm of acceptable.

There were so many things that grieved me as a child. My great-uncle recently told me just before he died that he didn't know me as a child, even though we'd spent a lot of time together at his home and on regular camping trips. He said he remembered my big brown eyes and that I was quiet and shy. This memory of who he thought I was surprised me because I am not a shy person and do not remember ever being that way. As I thought about it more, however, it occurred to me that I was cautious. I really think I knew that my family wasn't safe, and I needed to be on guard. It's strange to think that I was both at home and on guard at the same time. So my fantasy really speaks to my personal and powerful longing for a healthy family. It's no wonder I became a marriage and family therapist. And it's no wonder I worked so hard to break the unhealthy patterns in my family.

Brokenness and Love

My mother's family is replete with drug and alcohol addiction, physical and sexual abuse of all kinds, profanity, and poverty. I grew up among all of this. The family acted like these things were normal. They talked and complained about them but did nothing to change their lives. Mom had been a victim of sexual abuse from a very young age, and her mother was physically and verbally abusive and did not protect her. Needless to say, my mother is a very wounded person.

Cigarette and marijuana smoke filled our tiny home every evening. Most nights, relatives and friends visited to enjoy pot, beer, cigarettes, card games, and Raider football season. On special occasions, my mom used heavier drugs like cocaine, "crank," and psychedelic mushrooms, and I think she dropped acid a few times. I'm not sure if I'm using the right lingo . . . likely, it's not current, but it was in the seventies when I was learning it as a young child.

I didn't tell my friends about this drug use. Somehow I knew not to. Despite her drug use, mom volunteered extensively at my school and was later an instructional aide at a nearby elementary school. I just knew to keep all of this a secret—which, if you knew me in my younger years, would surprise you.

Though she is a broken person, Mom is also a very loving person. My childhood friends remember her as open, warm, hospitable, and a very good cook. I cannot tell you about my mother without testifying to her God-given gift in the culinary arts. She truly is a gifted chef. She literally "receives" recipes in dreams, wakes up in the morning, and creates new recipes. I have a section of my recipe box titled "Mom's." She says that food has always been her way of giving love.

Being the oldest of three girls from her parents' marriage (and ultimately the oldest of ten when you figure in all of the step and half siblings), my mother quickly became the family's matriarch. Her mother was definitely not the maternal type. While her mother was out all day and late into the evening, my mom took on caring for her two little sisters. Learning to cook full meals before she was nine years old meant she could provide her sisters with the mothering they were all lacking.

Cooking is the one area of my mother's life where she feels extremely confident and self-assured. When I was young, we were poor, but we always ate well. Mom tells a story of being a crack addict with her sister, Auntie Norma. Having spent all their money on drugs, leaving no money for food, my mom made a delicious "omelet" out of a package of Top Ramen and one green onion. "And by the way," says my mother, "it was a shrimp-flavored ramen, so we had a shrimp omelet."

My mom was also my biggest fan. Her ability for denial meant she saw only the very best in me. This was wonderful because she truly always believed that I was the prettiest, smartest, most talented, nicest little girl on the planet. If I had a problem with someone else, it was their fault. She would say they were just jealous of me or that I intimidated them because I was so smart. She really believed I was the best thing ever and complimented me annoyingly.

Mom sacrificed and volunteered in exchange for me to receive dance lessons and voice lessons throughout my childhood. She volunteered at my school and made sure I had good teachers. Looking back, I see that my mother's constant unconditional support, especially regarding my intellect, was a huge saving grace for me later in life. Knowing that I was smart and capable academically helped dig me out of some pits I fell into later in adolescence.

But Mom was also unstable, unhappy, and powerless to change herself and her circumstances. She coped by using drugs, overeating, and blaming my stepdad for her unhappiness. She exploded emotionally on my stepdad and my stepbrother, Michael, regularly. She was terribly unhappy with her weight and was suicidal more than once, that I knew of as a child. When I was a teenager, things got worse as her drug use became a serious problem, and her behavior decompensated drastically.

Quintessential Codependency

Webster defines codependency as "a psychological condition or a relationship in which a person manifesting low self-esteem and a strong desire for approval has an unhealthy attachment to another often controlling or manipulative person (such as a person with an addiction to alcohol or drugs)."[3] But I don't think the definition captures what it means to live in codependency. I read Melody Beattie's *Codependent No More: How to Stop Controlling Others and Start Caring for Yourself* at the beginning of my journey to emotional health. I was only nineteen years old then, but I still have that copy with all my reflections at the end of the chapters, underlines, and highlights. The information and the opportunity to reflect on how it related to me were life-changing. Melody Beattie outlines several codependent characteristics in this excerpt:

> Ever since people first existed, they have been doing all the things we label "codependent." They have worried themselves sick about other people. They have tried to help in ways that didn't help. They have said yes when they meant no. They have tried to make other people see things their way. They have bent over backward to avoid hurting people's feelings and, in so doing, have hurt themselves. They have been afraid to trust their feelings. They believed lies and then felt betrayed. They have wanted to get even and punish others. They have felt so angry they wanted to kill. They have struggled for their rights while others said they didn't have any. They have worn sackcloth because they didn't believe they deserved silk.[4]

This is a perfect description of my family of origin. The most poignant and obvious example of this played out in full color on a daily basis. Papa (Mom's dad) was an alcoholic. He died in his early sixties basically of alcohol poisoning. It was pitiful and ugly. My papa was gifted intellectually and was a great leader and teacher. He was a sergeant major in the army and taught JROTC after retiring from the army. His students loved him, which I saw as a girl when I attended one of his JROTC graduation ceremonies.

He loved his family, especially his grandchildren. We all had silly, nonsensical nicknames. Mine was Rooshkinga Appleseed Sidewall. The only tie to my actual name is that Rena starts with an R and my maiden name was Sidwell. Otherwise, it came completely out of his imagination. He was good with money and was successful in many ways. When I was in college, he sent me twenty dollars periodically and wrote me a letter encouraging me to break away from the family "traditions" of life.

Yet, Papa was drunk just about every night and most weekends throughout my childhood. When he was drunk, he was a completely different person. He would often arrive at our front door, literally falling down drunk. He'd stumble into the house, seat himself at our kitchen table, pour another glass of Jim Beam, and insist my mother sing for him. If Mom's friends were over, he'd make lewd comments and even grope them. Finally, he would stumble out of the house, sometimes falling to the ground on the way to his car, and drive away.

My mother would whine or complain, cuss and groan throughout these episodes, but she always sang for him and tolerated his behavior. She said "yes" when she meant "no." She bent over backward to avoid hurting his feelings. She never once called the police when he drove off drunk. She never once set a boundary of any kind—yet she was devastated and wounded every time he did this. She felt angry and betrayed over and over but could not take healthy action because she did not feel she deserved better—she believed she did not "deserve silk," as Beattie says.

Watching my mother's experience highlighted my longing for something better.

At first, I thought Papa's behavior was funny, but as I got older, I became afraid for him. Especially the time he drove drunk with me in the car. I experienced firsthand the actual danger of his drunk driving. My mother was angry and yelled at him, but no real boundary was set. I felt for her as I witnessed the depth of her fear and pain. She often cried and called her sister to complain, but nothing ever changed.

Watching my mother's experience highlighted my longing for something better. It was crystal clear that her codependent reactivity (although I had no idea of that terminology back then) was failing her and him and all of us. And so, longing led to seeking.

Longing for God

Living in this highly dysfunctional, chaotic, and often dangerous family, I knew intuitively that I needed God. I needed someone more powerful than the things I could not control to protect me, teach me, and show me a way out. I sound like a twelve-stepper here because I see the wisdom and value of the twelve steps. Anyway, at the time, I was young and had not heard of Alcoholics Anonymous. But I had heard of God and Jesus, and I had felt Their presence, especially on the back porch in the darkest moments of my childhood. I suppose that is how I knew I needed Jesus. I knew because my little-girl prayers for my mommy returned a validation of my longing and a sliver of hope. It's hard to describe because it was subtle, but I knew I was not alone.

Spiritually, my mother's family is Catholic. Nobody in the family actually practiced their religion, but Papa talked about it some. I was not baptized Catholic as a baby, but my brother was. My mother wanted me to be free to choose my religion. My family had immigrated from Portugal to Hawaii and were, therefore, influenced by the superstitions of the Hawaiian culture. Growing up, I heard many stories about ghosts, kapu, Menehunes, and various other Hawaiian beliefs.

My mother practiced being psychic, tarot readings, astrology, and the like. She had some friends whom I would consider witch-type people. I remember being sensitive to this, perceiving that these were not good things even though they weren't doing anything bad with their power. I think the fruit of their lives revealed the source to me. I know Holy Spirit was talking to me, and by the grace of God, I listened.

About God and Jesus, my mother and family were very open and believed in them. I was hungry to learn about and serve God. An aunt on my father's side was a Jehovah's Witness, and I studied the Bible with her. I was baptized as a Jehovah's Witness when I was thirteen years old and became very involved in the religion. I even "pioneered" for one month, meaning I spent thirty hours going door to door trying to get people to convert.

I think it was the rules of Christianity that somehow seemed plumb with what was written on my heart. The precepts of biblical living were in stark contrast to what I had learned in my family, yet I knew intuitively that they were right and definitely better than what I had seen in my family. I longed for structure and morality, so *Leave It to Beaver* and *The Holy Bible* became my guides. I decided early in life to do things differently than my family.

I remember being offended at an early age when my uncle declared over me that I would most definitely smoke pot, just like everyone else when I grew up.

"No, I won't!" I said, angry that he would say such a thing.

Years later, when I was nineteen years old, another uncle declared over me that I would be divorced at least once in my life.

"That's a pretty shitty thing to say to a nineteen-year-old," I responded. I left the house and went for a run, crying the entire time. How could he say that to me? It seemed like a curse.

I'd heard about curses as a child. Granny (Papa's mother) had called them "cubrant." This word was thrown around regularly during Portuguese-Hawaiian talk-story times. The stories were typically about some witch who'd become angry and put a cubrant on someone. I'd listen with big eyes to the details of how the cubrant manifested bad luck, mental illness, or even death onto the recipients. Also, my brother would tease me by speaking cubrant over me while gesturing like a witch casting a spell and then cackling in an evil way. So when my uncle said those words, I did not want that curse.

Mostly I was just trying to grow up with as few scars as possible. That's the main job of a child, I suppose. I was already dreaming up a different kind of life than the one my family exemplified. But just when I thought I had it wired, I found myself in a pit again.

Reflections on Longing

I invite you to consider your own life. This is a courageous exercise and not for the faint of heart. But if you're feeling brave or desperate enough, allow yourself a visit with your childhood memories. Take a breath, find some quiet, and answer these questions.

1. What is your "back porch" experience? Consider the people closest to you and how they impacted you.

_____

_____

_____

_____

2. When you were a child, what did you wish was different about your family of origin?

_____

_____

_____

_____

3. Describe a memory that points to or typifies your longings.

_____

_____

_____

_____

CHAPTER 2

The Candy Dish

I used to visit Mary for the prize of chocolate. Anytime I wanted a piece of candy bad enough, I would knock on Mary's door. She kept a candy dish full of chocolates on a cluttered and dusty table in her living room. I actually own that dish to this day. It's a tall glass dish with a purple hue. It has a pedestal bottom, and it used to have a lid up until a couple of years ago. I decided to quit guarding it, so I filled it with candy and put it on my counter. Someone dropped it, and that was the end of the lid. I treasure the dish because it reminds me of Mary and my relationship with her, lid or no lid.

Mary was always old as far as I was concerned at the time. She had long, white hair that she pulled back into a loose bun, using translucent combs to hold it in place. She wore thick glasses that made her light blue eyes look huge. She was fair-skinned with large age spots on her face, and her cheeks sagged below her jawline with age.

I would sit on this wonderful old rocking chair made of alder wood with a caned seat. It rocked so far back that my adrenaline spiked in fear each time it rocked back. Even so, each time I came forward, I chose to rock backward one more time just to prove it was safe. Before Mary died, she left me that rocking chair and the candy dish.

Mary had two cats—a Siamese named Ching and a tabby named Oscar. They were her "children." She fed them cantaloupe and asparagus, of all things. They apparently loved those foods. Every time I visited Mary, I would listen to her tell the same stories and repeat the same little sayings. She'd talk about various events she'd witnessed happening on our street and also about the cats. Oscar and Ching were always on her lap while we visited. I listened, but I confess my focus was on judging how long was an acceptable amount of time to stay before I could leave with my chocolate. It was only offered on my way out.

I think the chocolates were just for the neighborhood kids who visited. I'm sure I was the most regular visitor. I knew she was lonely, so it seemed like a good deed to visit her. And we had a symbiotic relationship because I had an enduring sweet tooth and still do.

When it was time to go, we had a ritual of sorts that we always practiced. She would caution me to be very careful not to go into the street, saying, "If you take on a car, you'll come out second best." The final step of our goodbye was cutting a bouquet from her garden. She let me pick out the ones I wanted. I loved the snapdragons. Mary taught me how you could pick off the buds and squeeze their sides to make them open their "mouths." Then she would pretend they were saying, "Hello, Rena." I loved that trick. I showed it to my children, and I show it to my grandchildren today. Once the bouquet was complete, she handed it to me to deliver to my mother.

I realize now that Mary taught me about sweet, simple community through this recurrent ritual. I thought I was visiting a widow, but she was teaching me. She taught me to care for and value the beauty of flowers, and she slowed me down to listen to another's story longer than I wanted and be better for having done it. I guess that's why I want to tell you about her. Mary was kind, giving, and grateful despite disappointment, loss, and loneliness. I'm so grateful she was in my life all those years.

Love Your Neighbor

Mary's husband of fifty-two years was named Glenn. She and her Glenn never had children. She said that during the first part of their marriage, they didn't want children. In the second part, they wanted them, but they just never came. As a child, Glenn was kind of scary to me . . . he shuffled slowly around his yard, and if I got close to him, I could see he was drooling. His speech was raspy and quiet, and I couldn't understand most of what he said to me, although I tried to be sweet and polite. He was well over six feet tall as a younger man, but he was bent with osteoporosis, thin and lanky when I knew him. His skin looked gray, and he did not smell good. I could often smell urine on him. Honestly, Glenn was kind of repulsive and frightening to me. My mom assured me he was "just old" and that I should be kind to him. So, I did my best and felt good about it. Glenn died in 1976 when I was eight years old.

With no children and no husband, Mary was alone. She did have a sister, Ann, who died when I was ten or eleven. As I write this, I feel it's important to include their names and a little about them as they have no family to carry on any sort of legacy. Anyway, when Ann died, Mary was truly alone.

At that point, Mary began to rely heavily on my mother. Mom took her grocery shopping once a week because she had never learned to drive. She started calling my mother several times daily for the company, mainly. Mom lamented the time Mary demanded. She acted friendly on the phone but would cuss and complain when she hung up. Sometimes, she would act sick or tired to avoid talking for more than a few minutes. It was as if my mother was imprisoned by Mary's need for her company. Obviously, Mary was suffering from extreme loneliness, grief, and likely clinical anxiety and depression connected to her losses and circumstances in life.

In hindsight, we could have rounded up a few more neighbors and organized weekly visits to share the burden and the opportunity to care for this elderly woman. We could have contacted a local church or suggested she talk to a physician for help. But Mom was unable to come up with possible solutions to this predicament or even consider coming up with one. It was the same with my grandfather's alcoholism.

We, therapists, call this "poor boundaries," "codependency," "poor self-care," and "victim mentality." My mom has all of these issues. I remember feeling bad for her, but I still thought she was being mean to Mary.

Mary didn't seem to notice my mother's hostility and continued to reach out to her daily. I think it was because she truly assumed the best in people. Sure, Mom tried to hide her frustration, but it was obvious to me, a child at the time. Mary seemed to see my mom through rose-colored glasses. She often verbalized life-giving compliments to my mother and regularly pointed out her goodness. Perhaps part of my mother's anguish was because she could not abide in a relationship where she was truly adored. Mary definitely loved my mother as much as she needed her.

One day, Mary told my mother that she was so grateful for all the driving Mom did for her that she wanted to buy her a new car. We'd never had a new car. Our cars were not even reliable sources of transportation. Family vacations usually involved at least one car problem along the way, parking us on the side of some freeway with trucks barreling by in scorching heat. Mary's offer was generous and life-changing for us. She told my mother to pick out any car she wanted, so Mom chose a brand new 1981 Buick Regal in metallic charcoal. It had plush seats with electric adjusters, power windows, air conditioning, cruise control, AM/FM stereo with front and rear speakers, and a cassette player. It was a beautiful luxury car. I was twelve when we got it, and I remember sitting in it in our driveway, just smelling the new car smell, enjoying the stereo, and playing with the power windows and seats. It was so cool.

Not long after that, Mary invited us to move into the house behind hers. She owned a lot with two houses on it, which was a common way of building when her homes were built. It was a small two-bedroom, much like the one we lived in next door. But Mary said she would pay for Mom to remodel it however she wanted and that she wouldn't charge us any rent. So we moved.

By middle-class standards, we didn't remodel. We didn't know what that was. We just refinished the original hardwood floors, painted the walls, sewed some curtains for the cute corner window in the kitchen that we looked out of while working at the sink, and bought a sofa, matching loveseat, and a coffee table. Still, I had a pretty little room with a brand new oval-shaped, sage-green rug that I got to pick out myself. My bed didn't even have a frame. The box spring and mattress just sat on the floor. I didn't know I needed a bed frame, let alone a headboard or footboard. I loved my bed with the comforter I picked out for it. I organized my small closet and hung posters of Andy Gibb and Steve Perry. Our little home was clean and fresh. I loved it. For the first time ever, I felt proud of our home when my friends came over instead of embarrassed.

Life was looking up, but then Mary's health took a turn for the worst. She was diagnosed with cancer in her eighties, and she knew she would not live much longer. At that point, she had her attorney sit down with Mom and my stepdad and arranged to give everything she owned to my mother! Having no living relatives, my mother was her closest friend and was like a daughter to her.

It turned out that Mary was very wealthy. Her estate was worth about one million dollars. I'm not sure of the legalities and how this all worked; I was thirteen at this point. But somehow, she gave all of this to my mother. This was literally like winning the lottery for us. In an instant, we owned two homes outright, stocks, and had a lot of cash in the bank.

It's amazing how someone's generosity can change everything, for good and bad. Mary fully intended to bless my mom and our entire immediate family with her gift. But Mom did not know how to live in blessing because she hadn't received the most basic blessing of a loving mother. That gaping hole in her heart blinded her completely. It stole her common sense, wisdom, and, ultimately, all of the money Mary had given her.

Desperate for a Mother

Somehow, the word got out that we suddenly had money. Not one week passed before my mother's mother, her husband, their five grown children, two of their spouses, and a couple of their children showed up at our house. Not to visit but to live with us. They moved from Hawaii within one week of hearing the news. You must understand that I hardly knew my mother's mother because she had never sent birthday or Christmas cards—ever. She'd made no effort to get to know me. I had only met her a couple of times in my thirteen years. I knew she was good at "talking story," as they say in Hawaii, and was a good cook. But she'd never paid much attention to me, or my mother for that matter. So when they showed up to stay, it was obvious to me that it was only to take advantage of my mother's good fortune.

But Mom accepted the situation and even seemed happy to have them there. They took over the back house, and Mom, my stepdad, and I moved into the front house with Mary. I feel terrible about what happened next because it was not right to Mary. I only hope she wasn't aware of it all.

Once my grandmother arrived, Mom began using cocaine. A lot. Turned out my grandmother was a drug dealer and began dealing it to my mom and the rest of the family, with Mom footing the bill! Mom also began remodeling the front house in earnest. She tore out the kitchen and added on a party room complete with an indoor jacuzzi and sauna, a wet bar, a fancy stereo system, and a dance floor. This was not Mom's idea, though. It was the idea of a cousin who just so happened to be a contractor. She was terribly overcharged, and the quality was substandard.

I was so disgusted and distressed by the situation. At fourteen and a freshman in high school, I pleaded with my mother to send them away. But she would not. We argued about this, and at one point, I remember yelling, "They're all a bunch of leaches!" My mother slapped me across the face and told me never to talk to her about this again. She said that she'd never had a mother and that this was her time to have one.

Mother? This was her idea of a mother? Someone who deals drugs to you? Talk about a warped view of family. I wanted out of this generational standard.

Mom had never struck me in my life, and I was stunned. I remember being shocked at the power of her dysfunctional need. I probably didn't use the word dysfunctional, but I know it was very clear that her need and accompanying behavior were sick and destructive. I wondered why she would willingly subject herself to being so obviously used. How could she continue to convince herself that it was some sort of love? It was all a big charade to me. It was a lie, and I knew my mother was lying to herself as well. But that wasn't the worst part.

Donna

This may be hard to keep straight because my family is full of divorce, step relations, half relations, and many children from various men. I used to confound my kindergarten teacher with my ability, at age five, to explain who was who in my family. I hesitate to title a section of my book "Donna" because I don't like giving her that space. But the fact remains that she was made in the image of God, and He loves her deeply.

Donna was my mother's youngest sibling on her mom's side. They shared the same mother but had different fathers. Donna was terribly sexually abused by her father and her brothers. Yes, these are the same men who came to live with us. And my mother knew all of this. Donna also had a history of preying on children sexually. When I was eight, before everyone came to live with us, Donna lived with us for her senior year in high school. She was eighteen years old, and we shared a room in our home. In fact, we shared a bed. Why my mother would put her small child in a bed with someone she knew had been sexually abused is beyond my imagination. Denial and believing lies are very powerful mechanisms. But I'm getting ahead of myself here.

One night, Donna got drunk, came into our bedroom, and began to molest me. By the grace of God, I was able to wriggle away from her, and I ran to my mother and told her what Donna was doing. Before my stepfather could get out of bed, my mother tore out of the room, raging at Donna, and punched her out. Literally. Donna was lying on the floor in the hall, not moving. Next thing I know, Mom is on the phone to Hawaii, screaming at her mother that she'd better fly Donna home the next morning or else! The cops came, and Donna spent the night in jail.

Go, Mom! And praise God that I did not stay in that bed. Praise God that I told the truth immediately. I am so grateful.

Now, six years later, abused and abusive Donna is living on the same property with us, along with her abusive father and brothers. Is the picture becoming a bit clearer as to why I wanted my mother to make them go away? Do you understand better now why I was so clear that this situation was gravely unhealthy even at my tender age of fourteen? I wasn't a rocket scientist. It was plain as day. Yet my mother refused to see the truth.

One day, I came home from school earlier than expected to find my mother . . . there's no other way to say it . . . having sex with Donna, her half-sister, the one who had molested me. This was so terrible and terrifying for me—very traumatic, to say the least.

Although I don't have any scientific proof of this, I wholeheartedly believe drugs are demonic. I would bet my life that I am right about this because I have seen demonic manifestations in action. People on drugs do things they would not do otherwise. I'm not talking about getting drunk and losing your inhibition and saying or doing something stupid or even destructive. I'm talking about how drugs can change who you are. People who were formerly honest and hardworking become manipulative thieves who blatantly feel entitled to take anything from anyone to get more drugs. Decent mothers and fathers become child abusers and sexual predators. I have watched intelligent, successful individuals with bright futures become homeless and hopeless.

Truly, I believe demons attach themselves to people who are addicted to drugs and take over their personalities and minds. I have seen this happen in numerous people, including uncles and brothers and aunts, and friends. They have become people I no longer recognize. And I miss them.

Needless to say, I was upset by the sight of my mother and Donna and all of its implications. It was at that moment that I knew I'd lost my mother to cocaine. I probably don't need to say how awful it felt that my mother was cheating on my stepfather with the very woman who had molested me, and it was incestual. My mind and heart were reeling. I had no idea how to digest this situation.

I pleaded with Mom to disavow the relationship, but she refused. She told me she loved Donna and had never liked sex with men. That declaration was followed by way too much information about her sex life with my dad and stepdad. I still pleaded with her for my sake to put things back to the way they had been. I couldn't believe she wouldn't do that for me—but she said I was raised, and it was time for her to have her own life. Looking at her life, I can see why "raising" me for fourteen years could seem like plenty of upbringing to her. I'm not sure anyone had invested in her for any part of her childhood. Still, I was in desperate need of my mother. The loss was gigantic for me.

From that point, and continuing for almost an entire decade, Donna became the "man of the house." My stepdad moved out and divorced my mother, my grandmother became the landlord and drug lord, and my mother was complicit in the entire situation.

Donna.

Reflections on Longing

We all have those people that choose for us how our early life is going to be. Children have little control over their circumstances. Sometimes it's a blessing, and sometimes it's a curse. Take some time to document the heroes and villains in your life, how you were impacted, and how you reacted.

1. Describe the characters who impacted the circumstances of your life. What did they do to affect your life—positively or negatively?

_____

_____

_____

_____

2. What were your impressions and opinions of these people and their actions? Why?

_____

_____

_____

_____

3. How did you respond internally and externally?

_____

_____

_____

_____

CHAPTER 3

Dad's House

When I was a little girl, my brother Jim and I would visit my dad a couple of times a year. He lived about thirty-five minutes away from us by car, but we rarely spent time at his house. To my little-girl self, Dad's house was so pretty. The living room used only on special occasions greeted me front and center every time I walked through the front door. Pretty wrought-iron rails lined the two steps leading down into the room. It was beautifully decorated, but the only furniture I remember was two bright pink velvet armchairs that rocked and swiveled. I used to tiptoe into that room when I thought no one was looking and pretend I was a princess worthy of inhabiting beautiful rooms whenever I pleased and sitting in pink velvet chairs just because I felt like it. Those chairs made me feel special in some magical way.

My fantasy was always ruined because I wasn't actually allowed in that room. If the house creaked a bit, a pit would form instantly in my stomach, and I'd hide in case Dad or his wife were walking by. In reality, I always felt like an unwelcome guest when I visited my dad. Apparently, his wife, Sylvia, felt threatened by me and my brother. I don't know why.

Sylvia was not only beautiful but smart too. She was a teacher at a local high school. I admired her keen sense of fashion and how she kept a beautiful home. I tried hard to please her. Except for sneaking into the living room, I was always on my best behavior when we visited. She was the opposite of my mother, and except for her cold demeanor, I wanted to be just like her. But she never gave me a second look except to chop my bangs when I was trying to grow them out, which I let her do without complaining, or buy me some article of clothing that she picked out because what I had brought from home was disgraceful to her.

She and Dad eventually divorced in large part because she refused to accept us warmly into their home. Dad has since told me that they would fight for the week leading up to a visit from us and for the week after we left. He blames himself and the situation for not pursuing a relationship with me and my brother. They divorced when I was twelve, so by the time things got really bad at Mom's house, they had been divorced for a couple of years.

Moving into Dad's House

After finding my mother with Donna and her subsequent refusal to end their affair, I knew I could no longer live there. So much of what was happening around me was concerning and unacceptable, and this was the last straw. In despair but completely resolved to go, I asked my father if I could live with him, and he said yes immediately. He asked if my mom knew of my plans and if she was okay with it. I said "yes" but refused to give any more information. I'm sure he sensed the despair in my voice, but he did not press me. He picked me up three days later, and I moved forty miles away and started a new school.

I was super angry with my mother, and I was distraught at having to leave all of my lifelong friends and school for a father I hardly knew. It was a difficult time for my fourteen-year-old self. Outwardly, I acted tough, smart, and angry.

About one month into my stay, Dad pressed me about what had happened that prompted me to move in with him. I was sitting in the extra bedroom when he approached me. I have no idea why I was in there. Probably just snooping around. The room was full of stuff that didn't have a place anywhere in the house. The stuff you're not ready to get rid of and think you might use again at some point but not right now. Anyway, I was sitting on the floor because there weren't chairs or a bed in the room. I'm sure there's some metaphor there for what was going on inside my soul. So that was the setting of this conversation.

He could tell I was very upset by something, and he needed to know what it was. At first, I refused to tell him. Honestly, the thought of uttering the words overwhelmed me. All these years later, it was not easy to write down on a computer. So to tell my father, with whom I was not particularly close, before I had even consolidated the impact in my immature mind seemed unthinkable.

Still, he insisted that to care for me, he needed to understand what I was going through. I appreciated his digging, actually. It felt like he cared, willing to enter my pit with me. At least he could see how distraught I was, and he cared that I did not seem to be getting better.

I finally found the words to tell him about Mom and Donna. Then I told him the whole story—about the drugs and my mom and her mom and all the crazy dysfunction going on over there. I told him how Mom had slapped me when I told her that her mom's family was "a bunch of leaches." I told him everything without shedding a tear. I told him with angry, bitter jabs and disgust.

"You made the right decision to leave, Rena. I give you credit. You're a smart girl. I'm glad you're here."

I didn't respond out loud, but I remember thinking, *Hurray for the smart girl. My life sucks!*

And then he said, "I think you should see a counselor."

"No."

"I will pay for you to see a good counselor to help you sort all of this out."

"No! I do not need counseling. My *parents* need counseling!" I love that sassy fourteen-year-old. That was a smart comeback.

Dad liked the comeback too. I knew he liked it because he laughed and said, "Well, that's definitely true, but because of the mess your parents have created, so do you. I think it's important that you do some counseling."

"No, Dad. I don't want to go to counseling. No."

After a minute or two, he pivoted and said that if I didn't want to go to counseling, he would need to see a shift in my attitude. If I didn't start engaging in life and lift my mood, even just a little, I would have to get help. But, if I could begin to move forward with some hope, he would take counseling off the table. I took the deal because there was no way they would make me the sick one.

I decided to stop wallowing and do something.

Moving Forward

Dad wanted to send me to a private school because he thought I would get a better education. The one we chose happened to be a Christian school. I had a hard time making friends there even though it was small and the students were mostly friendly. Those first few months were torturous for me. I wanted to visit my friends every weekend, but Dad wouldn't let me, telling me I needed to make a life there with new friends. I can see his point now, but it just felt cruel at the time. I needed my friends.

It's interesting to observe what people do when under severe psychological stress. I find it fascinating to reflect on the whys of certain behaviors and decisions I have made or those of my clients, friends, and family.

At this juncture in my journey, I made a big change, almost as a reflex. I don't remember thinking about it beforehand or making any conscious decision to do it—I just did it. On my first day at my new school, amid all the pain and loss I was experiencing, I changed my name.

I told everyone that my name was Regina. They believed me. Why wouldn't they? And everyone began to call me Regina. Of course my family had no knowledge of this. Dad's first inkling of my new name was when a friend called the house and asked for Regina. I heard Dad say, "No, you've got the wrong number. There's no Regina here."

I lunged toward the phone, saying, "It's for me. Gimme the phone."

My father was dumbfounded. "Why are they calling you Regina?"

"Because that's what I told them my name was."

"Why?"

Embarrassed and exposed, I answered sheepishly, "I don't know." And I didn't! I hadn't thought about it.

Dad looked at me like I was crazy, and it was kind of a crazy thing to do. But, hey, who wanted to be me right then? I sure didn't. I think I chose "Regina" because it combined my name and my best friend Gina's name. I really needed her every day to get through this time, and I couldn't have her. So, I just took her into myself by taking her name. Fascinating. It comforted me somehow to be Regina.

Two years passed before I let my new friends in on the truth about my name. Five of us were sitting in the living room of one of their homes, and I decided to tell them. When they got over the shock and asked why, I told them I liked both names, so it didn't matter what they called me. They all decided they liked "Rena" better. And so, I took my identity back, at least in name.

I am grateful for "Regina" because by keeping something from behind, she helped me move forward.

Moving the Bar

Dad was a very strict and demanding parent. Unlike my mother, he didn't make me feel like he believed in me or even trusted me. He definitely didn't think I hung the moon. Perhaps his view of me was more realistic than my mother's had been, but I also know his experience with my brother clouded it.

During the short time my brother had lived with him, he'd gone off the rails completely. By the time I moved in with Dad, my brother had moved out and was dealing drugs at a high level. He was running from the cops with a souped-up motorcycle on a regular basis. I know this because one time, I was on the back of that bike when the cops were pursuing him. It was terrifying. I really thought I was going to die.

I suppose Dad wanted to be sure I didn't follow a similar path. Unfortunately, seeing me through those lenses meant that he did not see me. I grew more hurt, offended, and angry.

I couldn't seem to please my dad. If I got all A's and one B, he'd ask why they weren't all A's. If I cleaned the house well, he'd add another deep-cleaning task. At first, I tried to figure out how to please him by getting good grades, making friends, and working hard. And honestly, I do think he was pleased with me a lot of the time. But he didn't show it.

It felt like the bar was too high, so I began to fight him about it. He'd laugh as I argued and told me I'd be a great attorney. When I lamented about how unfair his harsh punishments were for minor infractions, without fail he'd laugh, declaring, "It's good for your character."

I really hated him for saying that. If there's one phrase that typifies my father's child-rearing skills, it's that line. "It's good for your character" was his "because I said so" or "that's final." I couldn't argue with it. He wasn't going to budge; he never budged. That was annoying too.

But as much as I hate to admit it—and this is for you, Dad—I actually think being his daughter was good for my character. I couldn't win an argument. I couldn't convince him to change his standards for me or his way of parenting. So I had no choice but to prove him wrong, and eventually, I did.

Proving to my father that I was capable of making good choices and becoming a successful adult was a long, tumultuous process. At times, I'm sure it seemed his worst fears were coming true. Within two years, I had decided I could not live under his authority. So I moved out of his house without his blessing and lived with a friend's family for the summer. Eventually, I moved back in with my mother. I knew I could live however I wanted at her house. I figured I knew better than either of my parents.

I see now that no matter what our lives look like,
God is there.

Moved by the Spirit of Truth, To and Fro

Going to that private Christian school had an unexpected impact on me. I had made many friends and wanted to continue going there. The daily chapel times, the Bible class, and the connections I was making with the students and teachers challenged what the Jehovah's Witnesses had taught me. Turns out that everyone who isn't a Jehovah's Witness is not lost and condemned. When I saw the sincerity, truth, and worship of these Christian people, I disassociated myself officially from the Jehovah's Witnesses and was baptized into the Christian Church.

I began attending church three times a week with my peer group from school. We had a lot of fun together. I recall saltine/whistle contests at the local Wendy's after youth group on Wednesday nights. I had new friends and met God in a new way.

This sounds great, but church youth groups are full of people in bondage too. We were trying to become adults, and we were full of hormones. Of course, the guy most like my family set his sights on me. Honestly, I was not attracted to him. I had actually fallen for another guy—the smartest guy in school and a nice guy. But he dumped me after dating for only two months. When you're fifteen, you can fall in and out of love in two months. The other guy was persistent, and eventually, I caved. We began dating. It felt good to be wanted, and he definitely wanted me.

At this point, I started living two lives—one people saw and the other a shadow life that I hid even from myself to some degree. Still, God was pursuing me. I see now that no matter what our lives look like, God is there. He is in the mess. He does not stand far away saying, "I told you so!" or "Serves you right!" Instead, He uses every situation to draw us to Him.

The shadow life I was living began to look a lot like my family of origin—pretty much like my mother's life.

Reflections on Longing

The hardest moves in life can move us to a better place in unexpected ways. It's fun to see the hand of God working all things together for our good. Reflect back on your life with this in mind.

1. Write about a time when you knew you needed to leave a place. How did you know?

_____

_____

_____

_____

2. How did the Holy Spirit use a difficult situation to bring you into a loving community with Him and other loving people? Tell that story. How did this move lead to growth or blessing?

_____

_____

_____

_____

3. How has church been both a good and a bad place for you?

_____

_____

_____

_____

CHAPTER 4

Generational Jail

*C*oming of age in the early 1980s, I played the video game Pac-Man when it was new. I liked it. It was cute and fun, but I was never any good at it. I spent a lot of time stuck in Level 1. It began to feel like its own tiny jail cell. It never changed . . . the same loops, the same turns, the same ghosts. If I completed Level 1, I was proud. Level 2 offered new colors and new pathways, but I'd get bored pretty quickly, grab my Nehi Peach soda off the game dashboard, and head home without another thought about it.

The people who were good at Pac-Man seemed to know when the little ghosts would cut them off at a turn or when they would follow them around one more loop. They could get all those ghosts so close to them before eating the energizer ball, turning the ghosts blue, rendering them powerless, and feasting on them for high scores. I imagine they invested a lot of time (and quarters) studying the ghosts' patterns of behavior.

But I'm bad at strategy. Every time I tried to get away from those ominous little ghosts, they'd circle back to get me . . . they'd kill me, smiling . . . all the while. I needed a strategy to win, but studying and strategizing to beat ghosts in a video game bored me. I would have needed to watch it enough times with an eye for strategy to know the next move and eat all the dots and the energizer ball before the ghosts got me.

Strategy bores me in general. I'm direct and honest and expect that from others—something that has proven bitterly disappointing throughout my life. Sometimes because people aren't direct and honest with me, and sometimes because my blunt nature has been hurtful to others. It has damaged friendships.

So to better care for and love others, I'm trying to be more strategic in my relationships. It's definitely a weak spot for me.

Landing in Jail

Even though I didn't know my boyfriend was dealing drugs with my brother, I knew he was not the one for me. I could tell he was infatuated with my brother—his money, his things, and the illusion of his power.

My brother was a known drug dealer, but he was my brother. He had fast and shiny cars and beautiful young women. People often came to the house presumably for drugs and to show him respect. He fought a lot and always won, so they were afraid of him. Seeing all of this made me nervous. I knew it meant he was in deep.

But my boyfriend was a fan. So, when I realized he was in the relationship for my brother and not me, I told my brother I wanted to break up with him, and he said it was probably a good idea. That's all I needed to hear.

I felt strong the day I decided to break up with him. I was determined to choose wisely. I knew he wasn't a wise choice, and I was clear I needed to end it. I expected him to beg and cry to try and change my mind. I knew he would say mean things too, and all of it would be a manipulation. He'd already charmed, cajoled, coerced, and compelled me to do many things I had not wanted to do, so I knew what to expect. I was ready to resist any tactics he would throw my way.

I decided to tell him at his parents' home, where he lived, while they were at work. I figured I could just leave, and he could have privacy to deal with his feelings.

I was clear, direct . . . blunt. "I want to break up. I don't think you're the one for me, and I want to break up. It's over."

As expected, the waterworks began, the pet names, and him trying to kiss me.

"What about our families?" he protested. "My parents love you. You said you loved me. Were you lying? But we're so good together . . . I love you so much! I can't live without you!"

I was ready for all of this. I'd been manipulated by him for many months now through some pretty dark times. I responded clearly and with determination.

"Our families will survive. People break up all the time. I thought I loved you—maybe I did. But I don't love you anymore." He pushed back, continuing the tactics I was so familiar with, but I stood strong. "I don't feel good with you. I'm breaking up with you. I'm sorry. I don't want to hurt you."

Then he started to get mean. "No one will ever want you after all the horrible things you've done," he said.

I was ready for this angle too. "That's the chance I have to take."

"You're damaged goods."

"Maybe, but I believe God forgives me and makes me new."

"I'm the only one who will ever love you."

"That's okay. If I'm alone forever, I still want to break up with you."

He sneered, "You're stuck with me."

"I'm not stuck with you. I'm done."

Each plea and insult intensified. Desperate for control, his voice became louder, and his face closed in on me. Matching his intensity, I yelled, "I'm done!"

He slapped my face open-handed, and it stung. This was too much. I was not going to be hit. With fire in my eyes, I shoved him as hard as I could and turned to leave the room . . . the house . . . the relationship.

> I needed a strategy or I would not get
> out of this alive.

The next moment, I was flying across the room. I slammed hard against the bedroom wall. He hit my face again. I think it was with the back of his hand, but this was on a whole other level. I did not know I could be hit so hard. I crumpled to the floor, my cheekbone was on fire, and my head was pounding. My ear was ringing, and my neck spasming. I stayed very still and cried. In an instant, I knew he could easily kill me with his bare hands. I simply did not know that was a reality before that moment. He wasn't even breathing heavily. This was easy for him. I was trapped. I needed a strategy or I would not get out of this alive.

Cowering on the floor, I said I was sorry. I took it all back. The determination I'd been so sure of just moments before was nowhere to be found.

Abuse is so weird because, at first, he was on a power trip, blaming me for his violence. Then it quickly turned into a twisted half-apology. "I don't want to hurt you. It's just that I love you so much. I can't live without you. I was just so afraid when I thought you would leave me." He picked me up and tried to comfort me. Was he kidding?

He was not. He was acting like my savior. His touch made my skin crawl, and I almost threw up on him. I was quiet. I couldn't think. I wished I were smarter. Then he started begging me to tell him I loved him. He said he needed to hear that.

At first, I wouldn't say it. It was a lie. But when he became agitated and ordered me to tell him, I complied. I was afraid. Really afraid. I was trapped, and I needed a strategy.

The Judge in Me

I was determined from early on to be different from my family. Once everything hit the fan with my mother, I swore that I would never be like her or them. Yes, you're hearing lots of judgment and cursing in that statement because that was definitely the condition of my heart. As soon as I realized my mother would not choose me over her drugs and Donna, I began to judge her harshly. I believed I was better than her. I had no respect for her or her family. I was shocked and appalled at how she lived her life, and I told anyone who would listen about her terrible way of life.

Even when I was in the dungeon of the generational jail, I still did not see that I was there too. I thought . . . well . . . I guess I was in denial. I didn't even realize I had plummeted into the same generational jail my mother lived in. Truly, until I began to write all this down, I had always seen my journey as a separate path, even a very different path from hers. In reality, it was the same—same path, same place, same situations. Even now, I don't want to tell you about it. It's embarrassing. It's humiliating. It's shameful. It's the darkest part of my history. And even when I looked like a victim, I see now how I walked into those situations and stayed there. I know it is true because when I finally determined to change my life, I did, and help was there.

But here's the truth of it . . .

Victim of Violence

Growing up among family members who acted out and were victims of domestic violence, I had considered the issue. I always thought that if a guy ever hit me, that would be it. I would hit him back and then leave him forever. In the instant when he slapped me, I understood that reality is often tragically different from idealism. Suddenly, I was enslaved in a cycle of abuse. That first breakup attempt set a precedent for the rest of our relationship.

The downward spiral continued. On another occasion, he threatened to kill me with a kitchen knife. Somehow, I managed to dial 911, but he hung up the phone before I could ask for help. The cops showed up anyway because the call had gone through and registered my address to the police. I lied and said it was a mistake . . . a joke, and I shouldn't have done it. The cops came into the house, looked around, looked straight into my eyes, and asked if I was sure I was okay. They knew I wasn't, but there were no marks on me, and the house looked okay. I lied again to protect the abuser. I was imprisoned in some unseen jail of abuse, addiction (even if it wasn't to drugs), lies, and shameful decisions. I pretended it wasn't true. I did not tell anyone. We even went to church together. But it got worse.

I was stuck and in denial. But something deeper told me I was not to remain in this place. I credit this to my mother's steadfast belief in my intellect and capability. I am forever grateful for her gift because when my boyfriend berated me and called me stupid, I didn't believe him. I remember thinking he was just mean and insecure and wrong. I just couldn't figure a way out alive.

Larceny

It started when I was fifteen when we visited my aunt and uncle in Minnesota. I admired my aunt, and she was very good to me. One night, the adults went out, and I started snooping around in my aunt's closet. I found some beautiful clothes to try on, and they looked great on me, so I put them in my suitcase. I wasn't thinking. I thought I got away with it, too, because I had never heard anything about it. What I didn't know was that my uncle had talked to my grandpa (my dad's dad) about it.

Over the next couple of years, I stole clothes and food from my dad's cousin and diamond earrings, and a gold watch from my paternal grandmother. Somewhere in there, I also began shoplifting clothes from department stores, which culminated in getting caught stealing a pair of yellow women's Levi's 501 jeans from JC Penney. I was still a minor, age seventeen. I told the security guard that my mother did not have a phone because she was a drug addict and my dad didn't care about me (which I thought was true at the time since we hadn't spoken in over a year), so I refused to give my dad's phone number. I told him to go ahead and take me to juvenile hall. I figured I deserved that anyway. The guard took pity on me and let me go. I was shocked, and that ended my shoplifting career—nothing like a reality check.

A couple of months later, however, I received a letter from my father while I was in my second semester at Harding University in Arkansas. The security guard had followed up on my case and found my paternal grandfather's phone number listed in the phone book. My last name was not common, so he was the only Sidwell listed. I knew my dad wasn't listed, but I hadn't counted on anyone trying to contact my grandfather. Well, the Contra Costa County Sheriff's Department called my poor grandfather and informed him of my shoplifting incident. In addition, my grandfather knew about the other family members I had stolen from because they had told him. He had been keeping this all from my father, but when the sheriff's department called him, he told him everything he knew, and that's when my dad wrote me about it.

I still remember the pit in my stomach as I read his letter. I was with a friend, and I vividly remember how hard it was to act like nothing was wrong. I was mortified and exposed, and coming out of my denial forced me to look at my own ugliness. Somehow, I found courage and humility inside myself. I went directly to my dorm room, gathered everything I had stolen from my family, boxed it up respectively, and wrote contrite letters to each one, confessing, apologizing, and acknowledging that they might never trust me in their homes again. I returned everything except for the gold watch I had taken from my grandmother, a gift she had bought for her late husband years earlier. Regrettably, I had given it to my boyfriend, and he had sold it, or at least that is what he told me.

After mailing everything to everyone, I called Dad and told him I had received his letter. I hadn't spoken to him since I'd moved out of his house more than a year earlier. I can't remember exactly how the conversation went, but I know I confessed that it was true. He asked what I planned to do, and I told him what I had already done. He said I had done the right thing. Then he asked if I'd stolen from anyone else that he'd not mentioned in the letter. I told him about the watch I'd stolen from his mother but that I no longer had it. It was good that I told him because he'd asked his mother if she had missed anything after I had visited. He already knew. The truth really does set you free.

The only person who wrote me back or ever acknowledged any of it was my grandmother. She wrote me right away, thanking me for the letter and extending grace to me. She said we all make mistakes but admitting them and making them right when we can is what sets us apart. She said I was always welcome in her home, and she trusted me. I'm tearing up as I write this. I wish I could thank her for that now and tell her what it meant to my seventeen-year-old self. We weren't close, and I didn't know her well, but as I look back on that time now, I recognize the blessing she had transferred to me through that letter.

Thus, my thieving ended. I still am not exactly sure why I stole in the first place. The best I can come up with is that I was trying to get something I hoped I deserved. My mother had money and used it to buy drugs instead of paying my college tuition or caring for my other basic needs. My father had some money, too, and he didn't help with my college or basic needs either. So I think the theft came from anger and lack.

Lawful Homicide

I attended Harding University in Arkansas in the fall of 1985. I had wanted to go to Pepperdine University, but I didn't know the first thing about applying to college, getting financial aid . . . nothing. So when my friends were receiving acceptance letters, I was embarrassed to realize that it was too late—I had missed the deadlines. My high school best friend and my boyfriend (yes, the same one) were going to Harding University. It turned out that Harding would accept late applications, so I filled one out in late July and headed to Arkansas with them in mid-August.

While at Harding, I got pregnant. I had no idea at first. I thought I had the flu because I felt terrible all the time. I went to the doctor because I wasn't getting better. When the doctor told me I was pregnant, the world morphed into slow motion. I couldn't hear clearly. I was yanked out of the picture so that a part of me was watching from a distance. I felt like some kind of zombie half-dead. The next thing I remember, I was telling my boyfriend in the parking lot. He just yelled the f-word over and over. I was still in an altered state, so I just stood there silent. He immediately demanded that I have an abortion. He yelled at me, saying it would hurt his parents too much if they found out I was pregnant and that I was selfish to make any other decision.

I knew I did not want a baby with this man. I honestly thought that bringing a child into our relationship and the world I knew, in general, would be abusive. I wanted to be dead myself, so I figured I would do the baby a favor by killing it. I honestly believed that at the time. I had always felt abortion was wrong. I believed it was killing an innocent baby. I still know this to be true. But considering the mess I was in, I relented to his ranting.

At the clinic, I refused the gas that would put me out or make me not care. I did not take the pill to relax me, and I told them not to use anesthesia. I felt I deserved to feel it. I shed silent tears throughout the procedure. It was a nightmare. When it was finally over, I did not take the birth control pills they tried to give me because I intended to be done with premarital sex.

Not surprisingly, I went into a clinical depression immediately following the abortion. I only got out of bed for class, and I quit eating almost entirely. I was numb, but at the same time, I was in excruciating emotional pain. After a couple of weeks, my roommate, Karen, grabbed ahold of me as I passed by the full-length mirror in our dorm room on my way to the bathroom.

She turned me to face the mirror and said, "Look at you! You're a bag of bones! You have to eat!"

I looked at myself for the first time in weeks. I had been avoiding mirrors because I was utterly disgusted with myself. Karen's love and passionate concern jolted me out of my trance for a moment. I saw my emaciated body clearly, and it was scary. I agreed to go to the cafeteria with her. It felt good to sit with my friends again. I ate a little and was determined to eat more daily.

My boyfriend disagreed with my decision to stop having sex, so three weeks after the abortion, he raped me. I begged him not to, crying and telling him he was raping me. He laughed and mocked me while he did it. I got pregnant again. This time I was determined not to have an abortion no matter what. He flew into a rage when I told him. He screamed in my face about how selfish I was. I told him I would give the baby up for adoption, which was my definite plan. He kept screaming at me that all I cared about was myself. When he grabbed me by the throat, shoved me halfway out a two-story window, and threatened to kill me if I didn't agree to an abortion . . . I gave in. So much for choice. Five weeks after the first abortion, I had another one. This time I loaded up on every drug they would give me.

No human strategy could save me. It wasn't until later that I realized I had to go to the Source of my power to strengthen my soul.

Stuck in Jail . . . Trapped in Level 1

There are so many sad details of this season of my life. It went on for far too long, and I made too many shameful mistakes. I hardly knew who I was back then. I guess that was the point—I didn't know who I was. Part of me thinks I should tell you every detail, but I don't want to. It feels like too much focus on the darkness, almost like glorifying it . . . like it's okay if you go there because you can always get out.

But the truth is, many people don't get out. They become statistics of domestic violence, drug addiction, mental illness, and crime. I'm overwhelmed with gratitude that I was able to break free. It baffles my mind, especially when I look at my life compared to so many others in my family.

How am I so blessed? Did I make enough good choices? Was there a supernatural intervention? Was it because I told the truth? Only God knows. He is the One who brought me out.

Yet, even with so much gratitude, I still felt entitled to judge others. Looking back, I wonder how I could have ever judged anyone. I felt proud that I was the one who had chosen God. That's so crazy wrong! The truth is that He chose me, and by some miracle, I was able or desperate enough or weak enough to receive the Love and Forgiveness He gave me. It would take my own daughter's fall, many years later, to finally humble me.

Pac-Man knew he must carefully avoid the ghosts until the energizer ball passed through him, transforming him into a fearless and powerful ghost destroyer. In an instant, he no longer needed to run and avoid—he could face the ghosts and destroy them all at once.

Those experiences and decisions almost ruined me. I was ashamed and powerless. Each one was like another one of those ghosts in the Pac-Man game—chasing me, haunting me, and literally trying to kill me. I tried my best to escape and avoid them, reacting in fear, hoping my luck would change. But no human strategy could save me. It wasn't until later that I realized I had to go to the Source of my power to strengthen my soul. Only then could I turn confidently to face every ghost and defeat it.

Reflections on Longing

Most of us have done things we're ashamed of. And if we're honest, we all have stood in judgment of others to some degree. Hopefully, you have broken free from your bad decisions or matured enough to grow in humility. I know it's often best to leave the past behind and not dwell on our mistakes, but today, if you're feeling brave and loved, why not face a few ghosts?

1. Have you ever found yourself in a "generational jail"? Take some time to chronicle that season of your life.

_____

_____

_____

_____

2. What have you judged others for? Write about a time you judged someone or a pattern of judgment towards others in general.

_____

_____

_____

_____

3. Has that judgment ever come back on you? Explain.

_____

_____

_____

This was an 80s photobooth photo of me and my cousin Chris when we were fourteen years old. I didn't have any photos of us when we were little, but I do have these two of me, which here taken during the time when Chris and I played in my backyard, and our families lived together in my papa's small house.

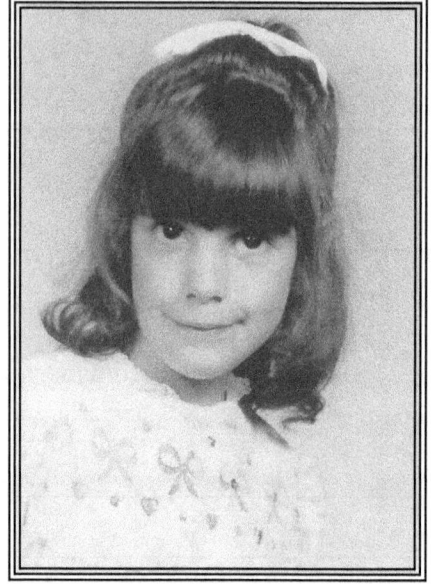

Age 6

Age 9

Me (18) with my papa

This is Grandma Vi, my dad's mom, with Amanda when she was four. She's the grandma I stole from, and the only person who wrote me back when I came clean about my thievery.

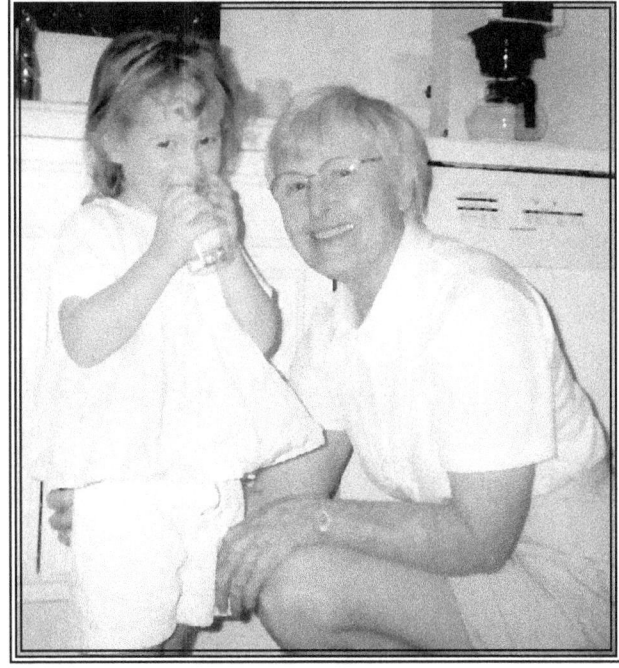

Me (26)   My mom   Cousins   Auntie Norma   Cousin Steven
                          Suzette & Chris

This photo was taken at Papa's funeral. My mom, her sister, and her three children, my cousins who lived with us when I was young.

PART TWO

Living

CHAPTER 5

Pandora's Box

I trekked up the steep hill to what was the top of campus at the time, where a not-so-temporary trailer was placed in the corner of Rowe Parking Lot at Pepperdine University. I had been there once before to get my immunizations, which the university required for all students.

I ascended the four wooden steps to the landing in front of the tan metal door and turned the handle to enter the small waiting room. Four oak-framed chairs with salmon-colored tweed fabric and a corner table formed an L-shape arrangement on two walls of the room. Across from them was a window where the receptionist worked. I let her know why I was there. A five-gallon water dispenser sat next to her window, so I poured myself some water and waited. In short order, Terry, my new counselor, appeared, introduced herself, and invited me into her office.

I cried through the entirety of that first therapy session. I answered one simple question and burst into inconsolable tears. Terry offered compassionate "hmmms" and "oohs" that are stereotypical of therapists. We make fun of that, but it really helped me feel held and heard. Intermittently through intense sobs, I apologized for crying so much. Terry kept assuring me it was okay and that I was doing well. I should just keep letting the tears flow.

When our time was up, I was utterly exhausted. That was my clue that time had indeed passed. Terry encouraged me by telling me I had done a great job of being vulnerable and real. She further observed that I had definitely done the right thing by coming to therapy, given all the difficult emotions I was holding inside while endeavoring to function as a college student. She promised she would help me through all of it, and we made an appointment for the same time next week.

I left that session afraid that I had opened the proverbial Pandora's Box. *Where did all those tears come from?* I wondered. *Am I really such an emotional wreck? Maybe I shouldn't go back. No, I need to go back.*

The second session was a continuation of the first. As it came to a close, Terry kindly suggested I start coming twice a week. I was grateful. I was beginning to understand how much holding I needed. I had no idea that so much pain and fear were pent up inside of me. How could one little question blindside me with a literal flood of feelings?

"Why have you decided to come to therapy today?"

I could've said that my best friend, Lara, had been gently nudging me to make the appointment for several weeks. I could've said that I was struggling with depression. I could've said that I had an abusive, drug-addicted boyfriend and explained that long sad story. We did eventually get to all of that and more.

But that day, I said, "I'm afraid I'm going to end up just like my mother."

Carrying That Heavy Box

It was 1987, and I was in Malibu, California. Through much help from church family and friends, I managed to transfer my educational career to Pepperdine University.

It's pretty much always a beautiful day at Pepperdine. The campus is set in the coastal mountains above the stunning Pacific Ocean, of which I had a view from my dorm room. The classes are small, and I could feel the care the professors invested in their students through their eyes and words. Campus Ministry began the semester with prayer and words of life to us about how we were placed at Pepperdine for God's purposes and to fulfill His plans in our lives. Even my work-study job with the Campus Life Office handed me a loving "mom" figure, Rita, for my boss. I had already made friends, some very close, in the short time I had been there. I was doing well in my classes.

Growing up, I hadn't considered going to college. No one else in my family had gone. I knew nothing about higher education, and I had no role models to show me or tell me about it. As a kid, I wanted to be a legal secretary. I have no idea why. Maybe it sounded more impressive than a regular secretary. I think I thought it paid more too. But when I moved in with my father and he sent me to private school, my peer group was college-bound. That's where I heard about Pepperdine, which was very glamorous and expensive.

After that disastrous first year at Harding University that I didn't like to think about, I returned to my hometown. I had rented a super-cool one-bed-room house with a friend, worked full-time as a housecleaner, and went to the local community college. Shortly after coming back, a friend's mom, Carol, began helping me find direction and hope. The first time she saw me after my year in Arkansas, she looked at me and asked, "Who stole your soul?"

I couldn't answer, but the words penetrated me. No one else had noticed, or if they had they didn't say anything. Simultaneously grateful and morti-fied, I was silent. I don't know if that was because I didn't know or if it was too much to say, or if I was just too ashamed. She didn't press me to answer. But she knew.

"Rena, what do you think you should do to get it back?"

"I think I need to go to Pepperdine."

"Well then, darlin', that's what you're gonna do."

She told me to call Pepperdine and ask for an application. When it arrived, she sat me down at her dining table and ordered me to fill it out. She was there to answer questions, but she made sure I did it.

I needed my transcripts from Harding University, but they would not release them because I owed them $5,000. My mother had promised to pay for my education, but drugs had taken priority. Anyway, I could not be considered for Pepperdine with that outstanding debt to Harding.

Carol brainstormed with me about who in my family might pay down the bill for me. She finagled from me that my paternal grandfather likely had the money. She didn't know that he was the same grandfather the Contra Costa Sherriff's Department had contacted when I was caught shoplifting the previous year. She didn't know about my stealing from family members. I could not ask him to invest in me or trust me with a loan! I told her he would say no, and I couldn't ask him.

"You told me you needed to go to Pepperdine, right?"

"Yes, but—"

"Now, listen to me. You can't go unless you pay Harding off. I'm gonna beg, borrow, and steal to come up with the tuition for you at Pepperdine, which won't be easy. I've helped you fill out your application and financial aid forms, but you've gotta do this, Rena."

"I can't! He'll say no. I can't handle that rejection." I sobbed, remembering vividly the exposure and embarrassment I had felt toward my grandfather because of my thievery. I wanted to tell her why I was sure he would say no, but at the same time, telling her the truth was the last thing I wanted to expose about myself.

"Darlin', you can," Carol declared in her sweet, loving, compassionate way, mixed with that Texas can-do attitude that says, "nothin's stoppin' us!"

She didn't wait for a reply. "Here's what you're gonna do. You're gonna call him up and say, 'Grandpa, I've applied to go to Pepperdine, but I cannot be considered until I pay off Harding University. I'm calling to ask if you would be willing to loan me $5,000 to pay off that debt?' All he can do is say yes or no. If he says no, then we will try something else, but you need to do this for you! Right now. Call me the minute you hang up with him."

I couldn't refuse her after all she had done for me. I wrote down her script exactly. Grandpa answered the phone on the third ring. My voice was quivering, but I contained my tears as I read the script. I felt sick to my stomach and embarrassed, but I managed to ask for the money. Grandpa was kind but serious. Ten minutes later, I called Carol back.

"He said he would think about it and get back to me tomorrow."

"I'm proud of you, girl. He's gonna say yes."

And he did. He drafted a promissory note that I signed. I paid as much as I could during the school year earning money babysitting. I paid one hundred dollars per month during the summer months. And when I graduated, he forgave whatever was left, tore up the promissory note and included it with my graduation card. I miss Grandpa Sidwell. He always loved me unconditionally.

I received my acceptance letter from Pepperdine, which I have saved to this day. Pepperdine was a dream come true and a place I felt called to for healing and hope. It had been a struggle to attain this dream. People had invested in me. I had worked very hard. It had been a painful, bumpy road to get there.

Yet even though I was grateful and sure I was in the right place, a cloud of despair hovered over me. Fixated on my existential aloneness kept me continually focused on my lack. It was wonderful that I was surrounded by people who cared about me and given many bountiful blessings, but my new friends received letters, phone calls, and care packages from their parents regularly. Nobody called me. My mailbox was mostly empty. My mom didn't have a phone number because she was living in a crack house. Truly, I didn't know if she was alive or dead. My father was absent because he disagreed with my decision to go to such an expensive school and said I would have to do it without his support, financial or otherwise. I coveted the family connection of my friends, which grew guilt and shame in my gut.

And then there was my past trauma and ensuing mistakes. I had done bad things for which I was deeply ashamed. The scars were deep. In my conscious mind, I focused on my lack of parental support, but much of the fruit of my family problems had a lot to do with my own choices and lifestyle, which were affecting me more than I knew.

It was my new friend Lara who saw this despair. It's so humbling to look back and understand that God was there, working circumstances together and putting people in place to help me. His hand is so clear to me as I write. I bonded with Lara right away, and within a week, I was able to move into her suite, where we did life together that entire school year. We've been dear friends ever since—family, really.

Lara could see a deep sadness in me and urged me to take advantage of the counseling available to students free of charge. I was confused that she would even suggest that, and I blew it off at first. She insisted it couldn't hurt, and it might really help me, given that my mom was a crack addict and my dad and I were estranged. I began to see that she was probably right. Maybe being unhappy was such a lifelong habit that I hardly noticed it. Finally, I listened to her and made an appointment. That's when I met Terry.

Finding "Hope"

Therapy unlocked a whole new world of solution-focused ideas, and I voraciously ate them up. It was like opening the box one more time and finding that glimmer of hope that Pandora found after letting all the evil out. Terry became my guide in breaking free from my family's generational line of addiction, abuse, and poverty. I had already learned a bit about AA and the 12-Step program during a family meeting I attended once when my papa went through a thirty-day rehab program. But Terry introduced me to ACA (Adult Children of Alcoholics), which had a meeting on campus weekly. I began to meet other students with similar stories and similar feelings. I was no longer alone, which brought hope. Once I stopped crying and was able to participate in therapy, Terry walked me through many therapeutic interventions.

Having worked as a therapist for twenty-plus years, I know I was a dream client. I told the truth. I tried every intervention and grew from it. Two things still stand out to me, and I have used them both in my own practice with every client that would participate.

The first was an early assignment Terry gave me to make a timeline of my life. I was to chronicle major events and people throughout my life in the corresponding year on the timeline and the feelings attached to the people and events. We spent a couple of sessions going over it. Her questions helped us gain a deeper understanding of the messages I internalized from the people and events of my life. When we had finished going over the timeline, she said something like, "Wow! No wonder you feel sad and alone and are afraid you will end up like your mother." That was my first moment of compassion for myself. I took a breath and agreed with her. No wonder. Having compassion is a powerful, curative deed.

The other thing Terry gave me was knowledge. She began to educate me about Bowenian family systems theory. Dr. Murray Bowen began developing his theory in the 1950s.[5] Before his work, mentally ill patients were removed from their families and institutionalized. The symptoms were seen as completely disconnected from family relations. Bowen turned that construct entirely upside-down. He basically asserted that mental illness originated in familial relationships and that it could be corrected in the context of that same family as the entire family became healthier. This was completely groundbreaking and offensive at the time.

Today, Bowen's ideas have so permeated our culture that we automatically see a person's behaviors and psychiatric struggles as stemming from issues in their family of origin. We say things like, "nothing happens in a vacuum," or "don't judge until you know her story." Indeed, it is so pervasive an idea by now that violent criminals diagnosed as "sociopathic" or "anti-social personality disordered" are sometimes cast as victims of abusive families.

Bowen's principles informed me, gave me hope, gave me a roadmap of how to escape the dysfunction of my family of origin, and eventually guided me in working with other families throughout my career. When Terry began working with me, she used this theoretical perspective to help her understand me and to help me make sense of myself. It became a launching point for me.

Family systems theory has eight major concepts that are basically ideas that Bowen observed within families. I grabbed onto a few of his ideas and ran with them. His first assertion that every family is its own nuclear family emotional system resonated with me.[6] I saw how my family members lost their individual identities trying to manage the anxiety of other members. It reminded me of my mom stopping her life and doing whatever her daddy needed when he was drunk, even when it hurt and humiliated her.

The pieces began to come together as Terry and I discovered together how virtually no one in my mother's family had differentiated into their own person. I decided I would be differentiated.[7] In reality, I had decided that long ago, but now I had psychological terminology for my goal. Because Bowen advocated for families, he called complete separation from family "cut-off" and did not consider it a goal.[8] On this point, I parted from him.

I felt I needed an almost complete cut-off from my family. It became clear that my attempts to differentiate were not "allowed." Instead, Bowen's idea of "fusion" was required. Fusion means that an individual must sacrifice her own individuality in order to help carry the family system's anxiety (addiction, abuse) for the sake of the family.[9] These concepts explained why my mom couldn't set boundaries with anyone in her life.

What I meant by "not allowed" slapped me in the face a few years after learning this. After many years of sobriety, Papa started drinking again. As soon as I heard the news, I called my uncle, concerned, wondering if the family was going to do an intervention to help. At the time, my uncle was using drugs himself. My mother had used up all the money Mary had left her, sold all the stocks, and was about to pull the last $20,000 out of her house. All the money had been wasted on cocaine. Agonizing over the situation (okay, I wasn't completely differentiated, and I hadn't achieved complete cut-off), I had decided to take conservatorship over my mother, take control of the money, and force her into rehab with the last $20K.

Aware of what I was doing, my uncle actually blamed me for my grandfather's decision to start drinking again. He said that my grandfather had started drinking because "of what you're doing to your mother." Papa never recovered. He was dead within the year, and some in my family blamed me because I wouldn't toe the line of the family rules.

I would be the generation that received God's love
to a thousand generations, those who love Him and
keep His commandments.

Another one of Bowen's concepts that resonated with me was the "multi-generational transmission process," which says that the way a family operates can be followed and seen to persist through multiple generations.[10] Yes! This was absolutely true in my family. I mixed this observation with what the Bible says about "punishing the children for the sin of the parents to the third and fourth generation of those who hate [God]" (Exodus 20:5). I took that literally at the time and set out to go back four generations to see what my forefathers had done to deliver such curses upon their posterity. I couldn't really figure that all out, but I decided that I was the fourth or fifth generation, and curses ended with me. I would be the generation that received God's love to a thousand generations, those who love Him and keep His commandments (Exodus 20:6).

I wanted to become differentiated, non-codependent, healthy, and successful, and I wanted to pass that on to my children and their children. I thought that if I did the work, my children would receive the love of God for a thousand generations . . . my family would be healthy, so my children would be healthy. I imagined that they would make good relational decisions, be successful academically and financially, and they would serve God—the end.

Terry also taught me how I was the "parentified child," acting as a first-born, which can happen with a large gap between siblings. My brother Jim was four-and-a-half years older than me. I was also the star of the family in terms of family roles. I began to observe myself conceptually within a dynamic system. As I analyzed our family, I was able to look more objectively at myself—at Rena, her roles, her responsibilities, her abilities, and her weaknesses. This helped me understand how and where I needed support to grow.

The time for that separation was right, too, because I was nineteen years old and four hundred miles away from my family. I was going to college to become an independent adult. I was surrounded by many people my age from varying types of families. We were all choosing our way. It's what we were doing as much as getting a college degree. Perfect timing.

Curious, Like Pandora

Having exhausted my family-of-origin issues, I turned to my box full of all the bad things I had done and experienced. I told Terry about my boyfriend and the extremely dysfunctional and physically abusive relationship we had. Discussing this was much more difficult because I had to be more vulnerable. I had chosen this relationship and had made extremely shameful decisions in the context of it. I felt free to tell anyone about my family of origin because that was their dysfunction, but this? This was my doing.

Every part of me wanted to close my eyes and resist looking at the patterns of my life that too closely followed my mother's. Maybe it was plain old pride. Maybe I just didn't want to admit that I was walking out the same generational garbage as my family. Maybe it was fear. It was terrifying to look at the part of me that *was just like my mother.* Everything in me wanted to avoid acknowledging that I was like her.

As I began revealing more and more of myself and my history to that point, Terry tracked with me and held it all. She helped me process each piece of brokenness as thoroughly as she knew how. She had me write letters to the babies I had aborted. I avoided that task for weeks, but I did it and brought them to her. I let go of a huge chunk of the guilt and shame related to those abortions through my work with her. I thought I'd finished dealing with that, but years later, while watching a video of the birth of my sister-in-law's first child, I was blindsided by another piece that needed attention. *Grief.* I didn't think I even deserved to grieve those babies but watching that video brought intense and unexpected grief. I ran out of the house crying hysterically, my husband following me to comfort me the best he could.

Abortion is so deeply wrong on so many levels. I don't want to make a social or political statement here. I don't want to judge anyone. But I do want to validate the pain, loss, and shame that women endure thinking it will be an easy "fix." There's nothing easy about abortion, and it breaks more than it fixes.

Terry also taught me about the "cycle of abuse," which is a social cycle theory developed in 1979 by Lenore E. Walker to explain patterns of behavior in an abusive relationship.[11] There are four stages: tension building, acute violence, reconciliation/honeymoon, and calm. We spent many sessions exploring my relationship with my boyfriend. She helped me chart the cycle of violence in our relationship. I was mortified to see how easily I had fallen into the same traps as my mother. The denial had blinded me. I was seeing it all for the first time, and it scared me. I earnestly wanted out of that relationship—*now.*

Terry helped me craft a plan to break up with him that would be physically safe for me. I did it. The plan was relatively extensive because he would always get violent whenever I tried to break up. But we were prepared. He was coming to Pepperdine to visit me for the weekend and see me perform in a show. I found a spot to tell him, just below Lara's dorm window, where she would be watching and poised to call for help if he touched me. I even alerted Pepperdine's public safety department ahead of time so they would be ready.

With everything in place, on Valentine's Day 1988, I broke up with him and never looked back. Those were some serious chains that fell off that day.

Me, Pandora, and More "Hope"

Before therapy, I knew instinctively to keep the pain and shame and even my own history to myself. I myself had become a Pandora's Box. I really wasn't curious. I was trapped, stuck, and locked up with all those evil things. To be the container of all those curses upon humankind had made me sick enough to need therapy twice a week, and that was hardly keeping me afloat. But like Pandora, I found hope in the box too. I found my own hope . . . and I found the Hope that comes with the knowledge that you are loved and supported no matter what evil exists within you or your history. Terry gave me that. Lara gave me that. And my church taught me that.

I became more curious and began looking in every nook and cranny of my Pandora's Box. I wanted to see and understand the dark curses that lurked inside of me. As I dug into the painful generational patterns and learned how to walk them out, my fear waned and hope arose. Having found the truth and the courage to look at it, I began to find freedom from the box and everything in it. I began to live.

> God's Love and promises don't look like our plans
> or will. Our answers are not God's answers.

It was time to stop longing and start living. Most people know living is hard work, and I was up for the task. With hope and a purpose, I would not fail. After sorting through so much dark material, learning how to understand how it all fits together, and the subsequent hope that was rising up within me, I closed that Pandora's Box.

Armed with the knowledge of family systems, my decision to completely remove myself from my family of origin system, and claiming the promises from God, I was sure I was breaking the chains and that my family's future was secure. And it was, and it is.

Yet, I would later learn that God's Love and promises usually don't look like my plans and my will. Our answers are not God's answers.

Reflections on Living

I was extremely intentional about how I wanted to live my life. I think that's the gift of coming from a dysfunctional home. You know full well what you don't want, but you're faced with the glaring question, "How do I want my life to be?" Maybe life is just happening to you. Maybe you've carefully crafted your life. Either way . . .

1. Write a few lines about how you hope to live your life.

_____

_____

_____

_____

_____

2. Get curious for a moment and consider what unresolved issues might be keeping you from living the life you want.

_____

_____

_____

_____

_____

CHAPTER 6

Elkin's Steps

I really wanted Jeff to ask me to Pepperdine's annual formal. In 1988, it was on Catalina Island in the beautiful Hotel Catalina. The top floor, where the dance was held, is a giant round ballroom with window walls displaying the breathtaking views of the harbor, Pacific Ocean, and majestic mountains of the island. But I didn't care about or even know how spectacular the venue would be; I just wanted Jeff to ask me.

Jeff and I were introduced by a common friend the day before classes began in 1987 on the steps that lead down to Elkin's Auditorium and the main part of campus from the dorms. We Pepperdiners called them "Elkin's Steps." The steps were only about three feet wide and descended diagonally.

I was heading down to the main part of campus for something. Jeff and our mutual friend, Greg, were heading up for some other unremembered reason. The steps were crowded with students bustling from one part of campus to the other . . . and there was Jeff. Super cute in his faded 501s, tapered and cuffed at the ankles, high-top tennis shoes, a plain white t-shirt, and his Levi's jacket also faded out. That was pretty standard attire for the late eighties. What caught my eye were his orange bi-leveled locks (a mullet), sparkling blue-green eyes, freckles that were out in force because of lots of time at the beach, and an adorable smile revealing a chipped front tooth.

As fate would have it, Jeff and I had a class together that first semester, Religions of the World. That was a happy surprise. I tried to save a seat for him and hoped he'd do the same every class. It usually worked out. He also took me to visit the local Hindu and Jewish temples for extra credit points. I didn't have a car, and he offered.

Then in February, we were involved in Songfest together. Started in 1973, Songfest is the longest-running student tradition at Pepperdine. The students form competing groups and perform original stage shows. Each group must create a skit with singing and dancing tailored around a particular theme. The groups only have about three weeks from the theme revelation to the performance. There are budget limitations, specific rules about how much harmony must be used, etc. I didn't know the details, but it sounded fun to me.

Anyway, those three weeks leading up to Songfest were intense. We had to learn lines, songs, choreography, and create sets and costumes. Everything. We all spent a lot of time together. It was standard to miss a few assignments or bomb a test during Songfest rehearsals. Everyone was exhausted but having a blast.

And there was a lot of flirting going on. Jeff liked to flirt, and a few girls were interested in him. Since the Catalina Island formal, or the Boat Dance, as we called it, was just a couple of weeks after Songfest, it was time to be procuring a date! I was not going to ask Jeff, but I really wanted him to ask me. So I told Greg.

"I wanna go to the Boat Dance with Jeff. Find out what he's thinking and tell him to ask me."

It turned out that Jeff was deciding between asking me and another girl who was in our Songfest group. It was a good thing I had Greg advocating for me. Jeff finally asked me the Tuesday before the Saturday night event.

I spent the entire day Saturday working on my hair. I wore the dress I had worn to my senior formal. A new dress was not happening . . . time . . . money. But my hair was going to be fabulous. I have great hair anyway, a thick dark mane. At the time, it was pretty long and generally beautiful. I really didn't have "bad hair days." But I wanted to really wow Jeff. I washed it early in the morning and put those squishy pink curlers in it by 8:00 a.m. Of course, I had to sequester myself in the dorm, so nobody would see me. Still, my suitemates teased me. I didn't care. I wanted to look gorgeous.

I guess I should've done a trial run with the curlers . . . but who has time when you're asked for a Saturday night event on Tuesday?

Unfortunately, when I took the curlers out, well, it just didn't work. My hair was a bushy mess, and he was picking me up in fifteen minutes. All Lara could do was laugh; my hair was that bad. She cracked up as I begged her to help me.

"What should I do? Help!"

She couldn't even offer a suggestion through all her guffaws. Meanwhile, her hair looked stunning! Every time I look at the pictures of my suitemates and me before our dates arrived, I bemoan my awful hair. I ended up putting it up, but even my bangs looked terrible.

I'll just take a minute to say this is an ongoing occurrence for me. Whenever I want to look really good, and I'm trying hard to promote myself, I end up looking not so good. Conversely, on the days I think I look really great, no one I care to impress sees me. I'm convinced God is trying desperately to tear down my pride, vanity, and female comparison. He's like, "Until your heart is completely stripped of pride and comparison, you will not look good around that person." I really think that's His game with me. It's comical. But every time it happens, it's a reminder that I am still comparing and competing. I say, "I'm still doing that, Lord? Thank you, Jesus, for keeping me low," and then to the other person, I say, "Hi there. You look so beautiful [Truth]. Have a great day! [Send a blessing]."

The irony is that Jeff had no clue I was having a bad hair day. He said I looked beautiful. The date turned into a weekend-long group date with two other couples. When I finally got back to my dorm, I told Lara, "I'm gonna marry him."

I used to take my children to Pepperdine periodically for various occasions. Without fail, when we came to Elkin's Steps, I told them the story of meeting their daddy in this very spot. Those steps will forever be special to me.

Several years back, Pepperdine redeveloped the main part of campus, adding an art building with a beautiful exhibit hall. Sadly, the redevelopment plan demolished Elkin's Steps. Sure, the new stairs are grander and very pretty, but I miss Elkin's Steps. Now when we go there, I say, "Here is where the Elkin's Steps were—"

"We know, Mom!"

The Relationship

Jeff and I began a healthy (not perfect) dating relationship. Again, Terry helped me through this dating stage. I had set some standards for the type of man I wanted to marry. I wanted a man from an intact family. Since every person in my family had been divorced at least once, I figured I needed my future spouse to know how to have a long-term marriage if we were going to have a chance. I wanted a man whose family did not abuse drugs or alcohol. Neither of Jeff's parents used drugs or alcohol at all, but both of their fathers were alcoholics. I figured his parents were what I wanted to be . . . a new generation free from bondage. I felt so strongly about this issue that I told Jeff when we were getting serious and considering marriage that I would forgive him if he ever cheated on me, but I would take the kids and leave if he became an alcoholic or drug addict. I meant it too.

I remember he asked, "You wouldn't stand by me?"

"Nope," I replied. "That's my line. My children will not grow up in an alcoholic/drug-addicted home."

I was applying all that I had learned in therapy. I was setting boundaries. I was understanding the relationship between my feelings, thoughts, and beliefs, and I was voicing my position and needs with the goal of forming a healthy relationship with Jeff. I guess it worked because we were married two-and-a-half years later. Once married, I continued on my quest to create new, healthy familial patterns.

On my first Christmas as a married woman at twenty-two years old, I set out to create healthy, loving traditions for my family. We still do them to this day. For instance, we each get an ornament and pajamas that we open every Christmas Eve. The ornaments are meant to be about something that represents our life during that year. Actually, I'm super bad at carrying out this part of the tradition, so it has become one where the kids make fun of the lousy ornaments I choose. I'm a little better at stuffing the stockings. Everyone gets a stocking full of little goodies and trinkets. I know stockings are a common Christmas tradition, but we did not get gifts in stockings at Christmastime in my family of origin. These were not deep generational-curse-breaking changes, but they represented the beginning of a dream for me. That first Christmas was like a Christmas on one of those TV shows I watched and fantasized about.

Marriage brought so many opportunities for a new and better life for me, but it was tough. Jeff and I immediately began to struggle in our marriage. I wanted him to show his love more, and my need for that pushed him away. He had fallen in love with the powerful survivor, confident me, and the needy, anxious, controlling, insecure parts of me were not attractive to him.

The first ten years of our marriage, at least, were a struggle, mostly for this reason. I remember complaining to a counselor several years into that time (I had actually become a marriage and family therapist myself by then) that I knew Jeff could be comforting because I observed him sweetly comforting our daughter when she was hurting. But he never offered me that side of himself.

The counselor reminded me, "You're not his little girl, Rena. He fell in love with a strong, overcoming woman. He doesn't want to be married to a little girl." She was right, and it wasn't fair for me to expect him to care for my childhood wounds. I still had a lot of growing up to do. I finally faced that truth and set out to grow up more.

Even though this was a theme of the first half of our marriage, it wasn't all bad. We learned to fight fair and, thanks to Jeff, established some important boundaries. I remember he made it a rule that we were not allowed to fight in bed. I could argue a point of offense all night long, which drove him batty. He wanted only good things to happen in the marriage bed, so he decided that if I needed to continue arguing, we would get up out of bed and go into another room to finish our fight. I agreed to this rule. It made good sense.

At first, I liked the control the rule gave me because then I knew I had his attention, and indeed, he gave it to me while we sat on the couch at 1:00 a.m. But very quickly, I would realize that I was tired and would have to get up early for work the next day. It also took all the fun out of badgering him since he wasn't trying to sleep. Accusing him of ignoring my feelings no longer held weight either, since I had his undivided attention. More often than not, I'd find myself saying, "Aw, forget it. Let's go to bed." The point of offense was no longer a hill worth dying on and only symbolized something deeper to me. My husband is a quiet genius.

Despite our challenges during those early years, our lives progressed in many ways. We found a nice home in a sweet neighborhood. I worked as a property manager and marketing director for a real estate development company. It was wonderful to be making money after the poverty of my college years, but I did not love the job. We began attending a nondenominational church in our area and got involved in our church community.

Becoming a Marriage and Family Therapist

About this time, Jeff's mother began pursuing her master's degree in psychology/counseling. She wanted to become a marriage and family therapist. By this time, I had ended my therapy with Terry, having worked on my issues with her for about three years. I found myself reading my mother-in-law's textbooks for enjoyment. The therapeutic interventions, personality development theories, and psychiatric disorders were keenly interesting to me. I had actually enjoyed my therapeutic process, even the painful parts; it felt good to be working toward health. As I reflected on how I had benefited from working with Terry and how I was often counseling and comforting my friends, I decided to pursue my own master's degree in psychology/counseling. I ate up the coursework, earning straight A's in my program.

By the time I was a licensed marriage and family therapist, I had two children. It takes a long time to complete those 3,000 hours of internship, plus studying for and passing the written and oral exams. I specialized in treating eating disorders, which proved to be rich, very deep, and sometimes extremely heavy work. Having struggled with anorexia and bulimia nervosa during high school and college, I took to it naturally and was very successful in my career. I am grateful to have pursued a career that aligned with my gifts and calling.

My Man

I have Jeff saved as "My Man" on my cell phone. It's not that I am particularly possessive of him. It's just that Jeff is a common name, and I have about three other Jeffs saved in my contacts. I got tired of telling Siri to call "Jeff Roberts." Jeff is a dying breed of a "man" out here in California. He can fix or build anything. I love that about him, except that it means he rarely hires anyone to do work around our house . . . which means that projects and repairs sit undone for far too long.

He's not much of a talker. He's calm, kind, smarter than me, and confident. I often know he's approaching because I hear his whistling before I see him, an optimistic habit he has passed down to our sons. No one ruffles his feathers. If someone flips him off while he's driving, he just laughs. He is not easily angered, and when he is angry, he doesn't lose his temper.

Jeff is thoughtful about how he does life and lives by his values. If you know him well, you know he has life mottos like, "You gotta have the right tools." He has used this motto consistently, so he owns almost every tool you can imagine. It's kind of ridiculous until you need some special tool. Then it's very much appreciated. I adopted this motto when I felt I needed a Vitamix (that $500 blender) or other expensive "tools."

Another one of Jeff's mottos is "only solutions." He uses this one on his employees, especially when they come to him to solve a problem. He tries to get them to develop a solution rather than just bringing him the problem. He applies this motto to himself religiously. Jeff can solve almost any problem, mainly because he sets himself to the task of seeking a solution, even when most of us would give up or call in an expert.

With me, he has tweaked this idea. When I come to Jeff with a problem I want him to handle, he often says, "Rena, you're a very powerful woman." I hate it when he says that. Not really. Well, sort of. He says this to me a lot when I express insecurity.

The week before going to Africa for three weeks by myself, I was feeling anxious about the trip. I had felt called to go and learn about Iris Global Ministries. Still, Africa was far away, and I was going without my man who made me feel safe no matter where we were. This trip was just Jesus and me. Of course, I knew Jesus was better than Jeff, but my flesh was anxious. I wanted them both. Jeff said it again. "You're a very powerful woman, Rena. You will be great."

Jeff's super strong. He will not be controlled. He does not bend to pressure. Another one of his mottos is, "Don't let it beat you." It's kind of a Rocky

Balboa thing. Once, he and Nick, our middle son, who was about thirteen at the time, were bringing natural gas to our new stove during a kitchen remodel. The steel pipe had to go through an existing framed wall. Jeff insisted they should figure out a way to do it without cutting any of the studs because that would weaken the integrity of the wall. After thinking and working to bend the pipe enough to get it through the pipe-sized hole in the stud without success, Nick had had enough.

"Dad! It can't be done! We need to cut the stud!"

I was surprised to hear Jeff shoot back with a raised voice because he rarely raises his voice. "Are you gonna let a piece of steal beat you, Nick? There are a lot of things in life that are harder than a little steel pipe. Don't let it beat you!"

There's really only one time I saw Jeff truly broken. We were broken together. That season was so painful on so many levels, and one of them was seeing my man broken. I cry easily and express pain and sorrow generously, so I *look* broken fairly regularly even though I'm not *actually* broken. I'm just feeling deeply. But Jeff contains his pain. Except when the pain involved his daughter, it broke his heart, and I saw it. It was hard to watch, and it lasted a long time. He's still putting himself back together. But honestly, I find the new Jeff is even better than the original, another facet of strength that looks gentler and more compassionate and humble.

Reflections on Living

Even if we are intentional, most of life is out of our control. Still, I think it's important to reflect on what we want our life to look like and how and why it's turning out as it is. Let's do that together here.

1. If you have one, tell your love story even if it didn't turn out as you had hoped. How did you meet? What was your courtship like?

_____

_____

_____

_____

_____

_____

_____

2. What are/were the recurring tensions or struggles in your most significant relationship?

_____

_____

_____

_____

_____

_____

_____

3. Have you created any new traditions in response to your family of origin? What are they? If not, dream about something sweet you'd like to add to your family going forward.

_____

_____

_____

_____

_____

_____

_____

CHAPTER 7

Bible in Bed

ornings in Southern California are usually warm and bright. Even when they are cold, the temperature outside is somewhere in the 40s or 50s, and still, the sun is usually shining. If it happens to be raining, the home is all the cozier. In a word, mornings are blissful in Southern California. This was especially so in the Roberts home between 2004 and 2014.

"Bible Time . . . ," I'd trill gently into the sweet little ears of whichever child had not already migrated into Mommy and Daddy's bed. All three kids would climb into our bed for the morning ritual. They'd each jockey for position as I would shift to be sure everyone had a cozy spot, reminding one that he'd had the spot by Daddy yesterday, so it was the other's turn today. Squeals and giggles would emanate as someone pressed their cold feet into Daddy's tummy or back, and he'd jump at the shock of the cold and groan. The delicious and oh-so-comforting smell of one's own children in the morning would fill my nostrils as I'd breathe in deeply, burying my head in my daughter's strawberry curls or one of my sons' necks right where it was the sweetest. I adored their flawless skin and perfectly formed bodies. I was grateful and happy. Blissful.

The ritual would continue as I'd open up the Bible to read the daily chapter. It never took long . . . maybe five minutes. Getting there and situated took much longer, and getting going afterward took longer still. But it was all part of our morning ritual. I created this ritual when I heard someone say that reading the Bible as a family every day would surely produce a blessed family. It was just one of many things I had incorporated into my motherhood routine to create blessings for me and my children and their children.

Daddy would usually sleep through the reading, which annoyed and hurt me. I wanted him to support my efforts by being awake and alert. Striving, trying, and pushing my goals forward, I made sure it happened even if everyone was sleeping while I read, which they sometimes were.

Hiding in those blissful mornings was worry. I was afraid that if I didn't do these things, my children would not be okay. I worried that they would stray from God's path and make the same mistakes I had made. And worse, I feared they might not escape them as I had miraculously done. Somehow, my fear clouded this blissful time together, and I knew it. I was ashamed of it and prayed for peace and more faith. But I wouldn't have that until much later in a most unexpected way.

"Train Up a Child in the Way He Should Go" (Proverbs 22:6 NKJV)

After five years of marriage, we had our firstborn, Amanda. Three years later, Nick came along, and then Joey three years after that. I was overwhelmed but working super hard to be a good mother. I read wonderful classic literature to my children every day. I attended seminars, prayed all the time, and homeschooled them. We regularly attended church as a family and served in the community through various organizations. We packed bags with snacks, water, and mini books of the Gospel of John that we handed out the car window to people begging on the street corners. My children were involved in a thriving homeschool community and studied classical piano, cello, and violin. My daughter taught piano when she was fourteen and made good money doing it. She bought her first car with that money. One of my sons excelled on the piano, earning scholarships to college with his talent. They competed in a national speech and debate organization and accomplished top rankings. I tried very hard. I worked very hard. I gave myself to my children and our family. We did almost everything "right."

All of this sounds sort of wonderful. And it often was. I made plans, pursued them, and watched them come to fruition. I should've been so happy. But honestly, I was more tired and anxious than happy. I thought it was the stress of living in middle-class America. I had grown up among people who did not pursue great things, so they were not stressed out about their work. The other homeschool moms pursuing excellence for and with their children seemed to do it with ease. Their children seemed more academically inclined, and the moms seemed more self-assured, more confident from deep inside somewhere. I felt like I was missing some special sauce that the other moms had.

Jeff had it. He didn't worry about our children's future, their education, or whether or not he was being a good enough dad. He had confidence, an inner knowing that he was enough for the family. Well, at least, it seemed like he did. But I was the primary caretaker and educator of our children, and even though I planned the hours, days, and years of their childhood, even after orchestrating the week-long California history field trip (and many other amazing field trips) and reading all the historical fiction literature and making a timeline, a salt-dough map with all the geographical labels, and countless other enriching experiences, I worried that what I was doing was wrong or not enough or not done with the right heart. I was struggling daily.

"Out of the Same Mouth Come Praise and Cursing" (James 3:10)

When my children were young, I wanted nothing more than to bless them and reflect their true identities as sons and daughters of the Father of Love and Light with my words towards them. I love the verse that says, "He will take great delight in you; . . . he will no longer rebuke you, but will rejoice over you with singing" (Zephaniah 3:17). In many ways, I did rejoice over them with singing. I showered them with love. I took great delight in them. But another verse from the Bible rang so true for me, "Out of the abundance of the heart, the mouth speaks" (Matthew 12:34 NKJV). When my heart was filled with good, the overflow was good. But there was too much darkness in my heart, and I failed daily because I was burdened with fear and anger that manifested in impatience and critical words directed at my precious children.

It seems so odd that the same mouth can produce blessings and curses. Yet it is so common—common enough to be written about two thousand years ago and common enough to still be true today. Even though it is normal to speak out of two sides of the same mouth, it is destructive to all involved. Raising children illuminated this problem in me.

I first realized that my tongue was a problem when my first child was about three years old. And it got worse as I had more children. It had been a problem way before becoming a mother, but I had not yet realized it. I could expound upon literally every aspect of my life where this had been a problem, including my marriage. I could see the look of defeat or shame in their eyes whenever I heard myself saying unkind things to my children, highlighting their poor decisions—they were preschoolers and small children . . . of course, they made poor decisions!

I knew my loose tongue needed to be tamed—I was in bondage to it. I recalled my mother berating my stepfather and speaking critical curses over my stepbrother. As much as I tried to be different from my family of origin, I could not attain victory over my tongue. When I read in James 3 how the tongue is a "restless evil" (v. 8) that "corrupts the whole body" (v. 6), I could relate.

I prayed and tried my best to get it under control. At the time, we were intimately connected to a church growth group. I regularly confessed and prayed with one of the women about my tongue and my anger. She prayed over me and for me. Still, I felt powerless to maintain peace and love in my heart amidst the chaos of raising children. One example that stands out in my mind is when I was getting frustrated that my son was having trouble blending sounds. I don't remember what I said, but my six-year-old son looked at me and said, "Mom, you're making me feel like a piece of trash." I was horrified.

How could I love, adore, and cherish someone so much? How could I need someone to be thriving and well so much? How could someone's smile and the smell of his skin delight me so much, and at the same time, I could make him feel like a piece of trash with my tongue? I wanted to cut my tongue out at that moment. Forget cutting tongues out for lying. I know that's so dramatic. But the idea of hurting my precious son's little soul . . . man, I was so ashamed and defeated. I apologized and hugged him. I cried and apologized again. I spoke the truth of his value to me over him, but the damage was done—I had made my six-year-old son feel like trash with my tongue!

"God Has Not Given Us a Spirit of Fear" (2 Timothy 1:7)

Before my children were born, I thought I had a lot of faith. I had evidence that God had taken care of me through many dangerous and uncertain circumstances. I boasted about His faithfulness to me, and I trusted Him to do it again.

Not being the engineering analytical type, I tend to make decisions in a nonlinear fashion. It's not that I don't consider data and possible scenarios; it's just that the final decision is usually a "gut" or "heart" decision. My husband, being the analytical type, makes decisions more methodically and carefully. I used to think I had more faith than him, based on our decision-making processes. Ha! That's so funny to me now. Little faith, lots of pride. That's me.

Fear is related here too. People say fear is the opposite of love, not hatred. I agree with this idea. The interplay between faith and fear is also interesting. Underlying fear causes us to doubt and, therefore, weakens our faith. Where there is little or no faith, fear abounds. So the two concepts have a reciprocal and inverse relationship.

When Amanda was baptized, she prepared a short speech to declare her faith before her father baptized her in front of our church. It was sweet and beautiful, reflecting her true heart. I was moved, grateful, and proud of her. After the service, someone came up to me and said, "She is perfect."

Without hesitation, I responded, "The jury's not out yet." Why did I say that? Looking back, I realize my fear and lack of faith were glaring at me. I had basically spoken a curse over her faith by that one statement. But the jury *is* out! And it *was* out! And it *has been* out! She *is* perfect! She was made perfect by the sacrifice of our Lord. She is completely complete. She lacks nothing. Yet, even in that poignant punctuation of all my prayers and strivings before God and Jesus's work in my daughter, I doubted. Wow. That's humbling even now.

Even as I was immersed in the joy of my daughter's baptism . . . no pun intended . . . it seemed I lacked faith in God's power and joy to sustain her faith and keep her close to Him. I did not believe she would be okay. I was still fearing for her future, vigilant about protecting her, and waiting for something bad to happen. Looking back, I see that I was so susceptible to that error because I had not yet given her to Him. I was doing all the work. I was carrying the burden of bringing her to God.

Of course, I knew deep inside that my efforts were not enough, but I didn't yet know that's what I was doing or that it was an error. I truly believed it was my job to ensure she was on track with the Lord. And there's the lack of faith. I secretly believed, "I'll do it because I don't really trust God." I was trying to play God in her life.

It looked like I had overcome my past, but my heart and mind were not free of the sinful, transgenerational family patterns of my family of origin.

I was given a prayer for each of my children when they were babies. My prayer for Amanda was that she would know her worth and always seek a relationship with Jesus. As I tucked her into bed each night, I prayed this over her. And then I told her about her worth but controlled her actions to be sure it happened. In retrospect, I see how my actions reflected a lack of faith and were entirely counterproductive.

Trying to make faith happen for her exposed my own hypocrisy and communicated it loud and clear. It looked like I had overcome my past, but my heart and mind were not free of the sinful, transgenerational family patterns of my family of origin. I was stuck there in the spirit realm, even as I was living a free life in the natural realm. I couldn't explain it because of what people saw. So I suffered alone, really, with this knowledge.

"Our Struggle Is . . . against the Spiritual Forces of Evil" (Ephesians 6:12)

All my knowledge and application of psychology seemed to be failing me. I often felt that I looked and acted a lot like my own mother. This frightened me terribly. It was my worst fear, the one that had tumbled out at that first therapy session: "I'm afraid I will end up just like my mother."

Mom's intentions had been good, I knew that. But she royally blew it. What if I was doing the same thing?

When I confided in others about this fear, they always reassured me that I was "nothing like my mother." But I knew somewhere inside that I was just like her, and I knew it was deeper than just psychological. It was a stuck bondage that bore the fruits of slavery instead of freedom. Henry Malone clarified this murky reality, defining it as ancestral curses or familiar spirits. He said:

> Ancestral curses are created by "familiar" spirits who know our family history very well. Perhaps they have been assigned to our family bloodline for hundreds or thousands of years. These "familiar" spirits transmit to you the propensities, desires, or strong tendencies from past generations.[12]

Malone refers to this battle that occurs both cosmically and within each individual and family line. This idea resonates so strongly with my experience as a mother trying to break free from the same repetitive mistakes of my family. No wonder Jesus repeated the words of the prophet Isaiah when He read in the temple, "The Spirit of the Lord is on me, because he has anointed me to proclaim good news to the poor. He has sent me to *proclaim freedom for the prisoners* and recovery of sight for the blind, to *set the oppressed free*, to proclaim the year of the Lord's favor" (Luke 4:18–19 emphases mine).

I had been poor. I had been blind both psychologically and spiritually. I still was, but I didn't know it, and I surely don't have 20/20 vision yet. I felt like a prisoner to the fears and impulses of my generational lineage. Their histories were oppressing me still. I lived hundreds of miles away from them. I had organized my life around completely different principles. Yet I was not free from the patterns they lived under. It looked like I was, but the oppression was heavy upon me.

I turned to God and the Bible. Right after Jesus spoke the promises above, He made a powerful declaration, *"Today this Scripture is fulfilled* in your hearing" (Luke 4:21 emphasis mine). I wondered why those declarations had not been fulfilled in me. I prayed daily to be free or healed, but there was no power changing me. If I was successfully self-controlled, I still did not have peace in my soul. I prayed and wondered why those around me also struggled and seemed to accept it. It didn't reflect the transformational power the Bible described. I was unsatisfied. It wasn't until much later that I grabbed hold of the truth of what Jesus said. There seemed to be only so much time for soul and spirit searching because of the demands of raising children, working, being a wife, and keeping a home.

So I just kept at it, doing the best I could and remembering that perfection is not a requirement in parenting. I apologized a lot and admitted when I was wrong. I kept high standards for my children and required strong character from them in work and relationships. For the most part, they excelled—all of them. I was proud of them. I was proud of us. Things were good. We had a wonderful time at home, in the community, on camping road trips, and during family reunions. We learned a lot. My children were deeply loved, and they knew it.

But my bondage was felt—by my children and me. I also knew the inside that others couldn't see. Even though there wasn't some heinous or abusive situation, I knew our family wasn't as good as it looked from the outside. I knew I was not free of my family-of-origin ways.

Reflections on Living

Many things come to us through the bloodline and patterns we have learned from our families of origin. I call these "familiar spirits." Often, they are painfully obvious to us, like a bad temper that we get from our father. But some fear-based heritages can seem good to us. Anxiety can manifest as obsessive-compulsive tendencies like being highly organized, disciplined, or clean. But even the seemingly good manifestations, if we get really honest, can have a darker source.

1. Can you identify a familiar spirit that continues to oppress you?

_____

_____

_____

2. Describe how it manifests in your daily life.

_____

_____

_____

_____

3. How have you tried to change this pattern in your life?

_____

_____

_____

_____

CHAPTER 8

Kingdom Streams

I had never seen a green sky before, but as we hurried back from John Brown University in Northeastern Arkansas, the sky was eerily green. My phone's emergency alert system warned us to get to safety *now*! The rain whipped us from the side as we ran across the parking lot into the hotel to hunker down in the hallways with the rest of the guests. My sons wanted to stay outside and watch for the tornado coming our way. "No way!" I yelled over the howling winds. The sky was mesmerizing in a way, and I understood their boyhood infatuation with the power of nature, but my answer was still no.

Once inside, we found children crying as their parents tried to comfort them. Mothers' faces were tense, their lips drew thin and straight across their faces, eyes wide, hyperalert. A tornado had decimated Moore, Oklahoma, two days before. Images from around-the-clock news coverage were still fresh in everyone's mind. Now we were in the path of another. We could taste the fear.

We drove through campus the next morning, observing the nonsensical surreal landscape of the day-after reality. Giant oak trees lifted straight out of the ground, roots intact, not a branch broken, laid to rest beside their lifelong home. Exposed jagged remains of branches jutted out from other trees. Their matching tops were nowhere to be found, carried away too far to be seen.

We had been in Arkansas for a national speech and debate tournament. It was 2013, right before Amanda turned eighteen. Nick was fifteen, and Joey was twelve. Tornadoes came through that area of Oklahoma twice in one week. Both times, we missed them by a day. On our way home, we exited Highway 35 to see Moore, Oklahoma, up close. The path of the tornado was catastrophic. I watched people wandering in a "trauma daze" around their once homes that had been reduced to a literal pile of sticks and stones.

I was struck by how much we invest in our homes and lives here on earth. I saw firsthand how it could all be reduced to nearly nothing in an instant. Not everyone can rebuild. And if you do rebuild, how will it be different? How will it be the same?

On the Shore

Sometimes after spending years building a wonderful life, it can be reduced to a hill of rubble in a single moment. An accident, an illness, or even a decision can change the course of your life, destroying what you have built. Rebuilding becomes key. You might have thought that the building was the work, but in reality, building your life is what you do from the shoreline. Rebuilding requires going much deeper.

When it came time to leave Arkansas, Jeff's parent's suggested that they drive our boys home to California. They planned to stop to see Jeff's cousin, Barb, along the way. Barb and I met when I was twenty-one, and she was nineteen. She was pregnant out of wedlock, and we bonded quickly due to the intense circumstance. I remember she asked me what I thought she should do. I responded with something like, "I can't answer that question for you because only you will have to live with the guilt, grief, and hardship of whatever you decide." Barb kept Missy and married Tony, a wonderful man when Missy was one. Together they had eight more children. Four of them were boys with whom my boys have a lot of fun. So my boys jumped at the chance to hang with their cousins.

At the time, Barb had been growing in her relationship with the Holy Spirit and spiritual gifts. This was a pretty sharp departure from the conservative Church of Christ teaching and culture of Jeff's extended family. Many in our generation had chosen to leave the Church of Christ, but most of us had chosen fairly conservative Bible-based churches. Barb was pushing the envelope as usual; in fact, she was pastoring a church called Kingdom Streams at the time.

While we don't always agree completely on spiritual matters, I know her heart hungers for more of Jesus. She has an appetite for God that I aspire to. At that point, though, I had not gotten wet yet. I was still on the shore.

Living Water

During that visit, Barb connected with my son, Nick. I'm not sure how their conversation started, but he confessed some very raw things to her, and she guided him through a deliverance prayer. The Holy Spirit fell upon him, and he was, as they say, "slain in the Spirit." It looked like him having trouble physically. He was wiped out and had trouble walking. Worried, my mother-in-law decided Barb had done something bad to him and would not let him go to her church the next day.

Whatever happened with Nick, by the time he arrived home, he was markedly and qualitatively different in a good way. He was humble, quiet, and gentle . . . peaceful. He was free of bitterness toward his little brother, something he had harbored for years. I had been praying daily for their bickering and fighting to stop. He seemed to have matured ten years in three days. Instead of a know-it-all, impulsive fifteen-year-old teenager, we observed a kind and gentle, transformed young man. Whatever Barb had done, the fruit was unmistakable. Jesus had touched him.

Jesus said, "'Whoever believes in me, as Scripture has said, rivers of living water will flow from within them.' By this he meant the Spirit" (John 7:38–39). Nick had living water flowing from within him. The Spirit had manifested a miracle in him. Both Jeff and I knew this without a doubt. We were humbled and grateful.

The first chance I got, I called Barb, "What happened with Nick?" At first, she thought I was also being critical. She asked how he was doing. I told her how he was different, and we discussed all the details. I wanted to hear all about it. That's when I started talking to Barb regularly. Nick had received living water, and I wanted it too.

Stagnant Water

Stagnant water does not flow. It's also sometimes called standing water because it is still and standing there. It can support life, but its stagnant state fosters bacteria and can easily become diseased. Water needs to flow at least a little to stay healthy. That's why the Dead Sea is dead. There is no sea life in it because it does not contain the resources necessary for life from a source of flowing water.

I have often felt that the modern church has become stagnant, even diseased. This may sound too strong to my Christian readers. The church represents a place of belonging and treasured support. My own history testifies to the generous love and care bestowed upon me by my own church. But a shallow dive below the surface reveals unhealthy currents. I want to talk about that part because what's below the surface matters more than what I see from the shore.

An old song we used to sing has a beautiful line in it about how Christians will be known by their love. The line is a paraphrase from John 13:35, where Jesus tells His followers, "By this everyone will know that you are my disciples, if you love one another."

It seems so simple. Love. Everyone can get on board with the idea of love. It's not controversial, even with today's cultural divisions. That was Jesus's vision for His Church. If we loved each other, that would be a powerful witness and point everyone to Jesus. Christians would be known for their love.

Or not. I work in a very liberal field. I'm a marriage and family therapist in California, and most of my colleagues are socially liberal with various spiritual beliefs. A few are conservative Christians, but most of those work primarily with Christian clients. I felt called to work with and among people who were not necessarily in the body of Christ. Through my work at a residential treatment center for eating disorders, I grew very close to a small group of colleagues. They remain some of my very best and dearest friends. As these relationships developed, however, my faith was often a topic of discussion and exploration with them.

They'd ask me things like, "Do you believe you can 'pray the gay away'?" "I'd like you to read *The DaVinci Code* and hear your thoughts on what it says about the church," and "Are you really going to teach your children not to have sex before marriage? How will they know if they are sexually compatible?"

These discussions watered the questions growing in my own heart and mind. My questions were less culturally based and more centered on the power of Christ to transform, especially among the body of Christ. I asked myself things like, why is there so much gossip among my church family? Why is there so much competition among church members and leaders? Why do Christians judge each other? Why do we judge non-Christians for living non-Christian lifestyles or holding a worldview contrary to the Bible? Why do Christians flip off people while driving, sometimes in the church parking lot? Why do Christians have sex while dating? Why are Christians gripped with anxiety disorders, depression, obsessive-compulsive disorders, and a whole array of psychological pathology? Why do pastors have affairs and destroy their families? Why do pastors steal from the church? Why do youth church leaders sexually abuse the youth in their programs? And why would church leadership attempt to cover up any of these things?

I would say these are signs of disease.

And for me, personally—why do I speak so often in an ugly tone to my husband? Why am I so afraid that my children will be damaged if I'm not super careful with them? Why do I gossip? Why do I hold onto offenses and unforgiveness toward others who've hurt me? Why don't I have self-control?

I would pray daily for the ability not to do these things. The Bible says that we are a new creation in Christ (2 Corinthians 5:17). It says that the old is gone, and the new has come. Why was I continuing in the same old sin every single day?

The Bible also says that the fruit of the Spirit is love, joy, peace, patience, kindness, goodness, faithfulness, and self-control (Galatians 5:22–23). I literally painted that Scripture on the wall above my dining room table so I could see it all day, every day. So why, please tell me, did I struggle to love people? Why did I struggle with a depressed mood? Why did I lack joy? Why did I struggle with worry and fear as I raised my children? Why was I so impatient? Why was I short-tempered, unkind, and rough in my speech to my children? Why did I lack faith and struggle to trust God? And why, why, why was I unable to control myself despite really, really wanting to?

I knew this meant I was walking by the flesh and not in the Spirit. Living water was not flowing within me. Clearly, I was not manifesting the fruit of the Spirit. Why not? I prayed more. I confessed it to close Christian sisters. We prayed together often because they had the same struggles. So why? Why were we all struggling with similar sins? None of us, it would appear, had the Spirit flowing through us. Neither did pretty much any other Christian person I knew.

We would excuse ourselves, saying it's because we weren't perfect on this side of heaven. We would say we're a work in progress. But that does not agree with the Bible. The Bible says we are a new creation (2 Corinthians 5:17). The Bible says Jesus came to set us free from sin (Romans 6:18–22). The Bible says we would do greater things than Jesus (John 14:12–14). The Bible says our love would set us apart as Christians (John 13:35). The Bible says we are being transformed by the renewing of our minds (Romans 12:2).

I'm not saying I didn't see any transformation. Testimonies of people turning their lives around in a moment are sure. My own mother was set completely free from a crack cocaine addiction instantly. That was a miracle and a gift from God, most certainly. But seven years later, she was an alcoholic, living in denial, lying and manipulating, full of fear and even hatred. That was not a transformation.

Why not? Why aren't Christians becoming like Christ? Christ-ones? That's what the word means. Sadly, I did not see this happening. The church smelled bad. It was just sitting there, barely keeping its people afloat. I didn't see it flowing and overflowing with life.

And as much as I wanted it for myself, I did not have the living water of God flowing through me. I was so frustrated with this fact. It caused me to doubt Christianity, frankly. When my colleagues pointed out the hypocrisy, I couldn't deny it. So in my thirties, I began a deep dive into the study of apologetics. And although I agreed with the tenets of apologetics and decided Christianity is true, I continued to be frustrated by the rotten fruit of most Christians, including myself. Because of this, I did not want to defend its truth to my colleagues.

Facts seemed to me not as powerful as the proof of personal transformation. I thought, and still think, that if Christians truly walked this planet as Christ-ones—Christ, who said the kingdom of God was at hand (Mark 1:15) because He took the kingdom of God everywhere He went . . . Christ, who said that anyone who had seen Him had seen the Father (John 14:9–11) . . . Christ, who said that He would inhabit anyone who believed in Him (John 14:20)—if we walked this planet truly manifesting Christ in us, people would be streaming to our churches. It would be like when Christ walked the earth, and the crowds pressed in on Him everywhere He went (Luke 5:1). They were starved for the kind of love, truth, and peace He brought.

I was frustrated that we didn't see miracles too. Jesus said we would do greater things than He did (John 14:12–14). Really? When?

Flowing water is clean and clear. Stagnant water is often green and opaque, much like the lack of transparency I saw in church leadership. The goal seemed only to present a certain image that churchgoers would like so they would keep coming and financially supporting the church. That did not seem like the Spirit of truth and faith to me. That seemed like fear and deceit. It was sick, and it made me feel sick.

I'm sharing my frustrations here only to inform you of the soil of my heart. I do not want to judge the church or anyone in it. I love God's church and the people in it. I was equally frustrated with my own smelly water. But I was looking for another way. It didn't seem right that we should all belong to this Christian club, continue living by our flesh, and be plagued spiritually.

One of my most beloved Christian examples is Corrie ten Boom. I read her book *The Hiding Place* in 2002. Now that woman and her sister, Betsy, gave me a picture and example of walking by the Spirit in love. Hers is a powerful story of a humble Christian family living in Holland during the Nazi occupation of Holland. Corrie inspires me with her example of supernatural faith, forgiving the worst offenses, choosing to love her enemy, and abiding in intimacy with God.

What if every Christian—or even half of us!—carried what Corrie carried? What if Jesus was truly in us and our lives truly reflected His love? What if we went deep and dug trenches from our stagnant pools straight to the streams that flow from the throne of God? His water is the "river of the water of life, as clear as crystal" (Revelation 22:1).

That's what I saw in Nick that day. I was hungry for the power of the Holy Spirit to change me. I ached for that miraculous transformation I saw in my son. Despite years of prayer and effort, I was unchanged. I wanted what Nick had, so I began a faith walk with Barb.

Deep Waters

It's tough to describe what Barb did with me, what she gave me, and how it happened exactly. Before I began my journey with Barb, I had studied and been a part of every aspect of Christian discipleship and mentoring. All of these activities were supportive and lovely, but they didn't bring transformation and real freedom in Christ. They pointed me to Jesus, but I could not receive Him fully. Somehow Barb's methods were different, and they changed my heart.

Barb said she was "walking with me." I like this phrase because it implies being together, not just meeting periodically. It implies doing life together and sharing intimately.

I have a friend whom I have literally walked with for over ten years. We walk from 5:00 to 6:00 a.m. every morning. When you spend an uninterrupted hour with someone five days a week, you know intimate details of each other's lives. Judy knows all about my transformation process. She has watched me go from pain, fear, and anger to joy, faith, and love. She's watched anxiety and judgment melt off me. And she knows it wasn't momentary because she has seen firsthand how painful, difficult situations no longer defeat me. She's watched me trust God through situations that would scare any mother half to death. Judy knows me better than almost anyone.

So just like Judy, Barbara was walking with me, too, only spiritually. She wanted to know both the big and little things in my mind and heart. We put each thought, attitude, and pattern of behavior under the light of Jesus and asked Holy Spirit to guide us into truth. It wasn't a counseling session because I was having some issues. She walked with me through my life—past, present, and future, looking in the corners and crevices. She also told me God would bring people for me to "walk with," and I should pray for this to happen.

Barbara knows freedom is real and attainable. She taught me about "Sozo" (from *soteria*, Greek for salvation). That salvation means we can truly be made whole, delivered from afflictions, healed . . . *transformed* by the power of the Holy Spirit. Jesus came to set the captives free (Luke 4:18), for real. She infused this knowledge into me. At first, in little ways, we simply expected freedom and transformation to happen every time we prayed. She'd ask, "What's different?" or "What are you noticing?" She'd point my focus to what Holy Spirit was showing me and doing in me. It reminds me of that famous hymn by Helen Lemmel, "Turn your eyes upon Jesus. Look full in

His wonderful face. And the things of earth will grow strangely dim, in the light of His glory and grace."[13]

I began to live those words out in my daily life because Barbara taught me to focus on Christ and heavenly realities. She taught me a new way to pray. It seemed like every question I had about life or direction or problems, her response was the same: "Ask Holy Spirit." It's a conversation. We began having these lovely, meandering conversations with Holy Spirit that surprised me over and over. That's how I knew the thoughts were not my own. She taught me how to pray in a way that is somewhat systematic or formulated but also free-flowing, like the best therapy session ever. Pray and listen and engage. "What are you feeling, sensing, hearing?"

Walking out your freedom is becoming aware of all the ways you are held captive and then addressing those, moment to moment, with Holy Spirit.

She also taught me about walking out deliverance and working out my salvation. This is a huge concept that I will show in more detail later. If you do not walk out your freedom, you won't be free. Walking out deliverance or freedom means that you live as though you were free. It's more than fake-it-till-you-make-it, though. It's deeper. Jesus literally walked with His disciples from place to place for three years. We know of only a few of their conversations. Several of them were challenging and pierced straight to the motivations of the disciples' hearts. That's the kind of walking I'm referring to. They could not hide their hearts from Jesus, let alone their actions when walking and living together 24/7.

Similarly, walking out your freedom is becoming aware of all the ways you are held captive and then addressing those, moment to moment, with Holy Spirit. It's almost like cognitive behavioral therapy with Jesus. Maybe you pray for deliverance from the root of bitterness in your heart. You pray through forgiveness and repentance, and blessing. Then, an hour later or a day later, or a year later, something happens that triggers that nasty bitterness. For me, it was more like ten minutes later.

Walking out that deliverance means I immediately take that trigger to Jesus, pray through it again, align my will to His will, my life to His kingdom, and then walk in forgiveness, grace, and mercy. The moment a thought comes that is not in alignment with love and kingdom, I take it captive and conform it to love. Barbara was a hard teacher of this necessity. She really didn't give me any slack. You'll see this as you continue to read. I am grateful for how she continuously challenged me to walk out my freedom.

If I had to name the one most important thing Barb taught me, it would be a new type of relationship with God. I've been alluding to it by describing the *things* she taught me: freedom is real on earth, deeper and listening prayer, Sozo, and Holy Spirit focus. But if I had to use just one word, I would say it's "relationship." She introduced me to a different kind of relationship with God.

And offered a different type of mentorship. It wasn't a religious, rule-following, structured type of mentorship. She reached out to me every couple of days, "Are you good? I'm praying for you." And she did pray for me.

I regularly received texts like, "I've been praying for you, and the Lord gave me a word for you." I was quick to return those texts. Who doesn't want to hear what the Lord is saying about you? She often recommended books and various teachings that had been meaningful to her. Sometimes I did not take them for months after her first recommendation. She wouldn't fret about it at all. It would just come up organically as we talked through some areas where I continued to get snagged. She'd say, "I really want to encourage you to read _____ (for the eighth time). I think it will really bless you."

Finally! I was moving forward with God. I was finding what had been lacking in my church experience so far. I was getting all of this teaching about God's goodness and power alive in us to transform us. It was fun and exciting. Finally, a group of Christians who were seeking and manifesting the type of relationship with God I had been hungering and thirsting for.

And then, on my daughter's eighteenth birthday, it all came crashing down.

Reflections on Living

If you've ever backpacked in the mountains, you know there's nothing better than a dip in a clean mountain river after a long hot hike through the wilderness. Except for maybe finding a clean stream when you've run out of drinking water or taking in the splendor of a huge waterfall displaying the majestic power and beauty of flowing water. Water itself is wonderful, and it's a perfect metaphor for our journey through life. With this in mind, meditate on these questions.

1. What areas of your life are stagnant? What patterns stink like a stagnant pond or infected wound in your life?

_____

_____

_____

_____

_____

_____

2. What is damming up the flow of freedom?

_____

_____

_____

_____

_____

3. How might you feel and act differently if love flowed freely within and through you?

_____

_____

_____

_____

_____

_____

CHAPTER 9

Revelations at the Beach

anta Claus Beach is a gorgeous stretch of beach located between Ventura and Santa Barbara. It doesn't seem to be in any city. It's just an exit off Highway 101 with the same name. There are a couple of shops and a restaurant with outdoor seating on the sand. I've spent countless afternoons there, sharing dreams and setbacks with my dear and powerful friend Jessica, who also happens to be an amazing psychotherapist.

Sometimes beaches are foggy, especially in Northern California, where I grew up. Santa Claus Beach wasn't foggy that day—it was its glorious sunny self. But I was foggy. I was, in fact, lost in a fog, the dense kind where you can't see your own hand in front of your face. Do I have a hand? Am I really here? I can't see anything! I was disoriented. Lost. Afraid.

Fog does that. When the clouds are high and far away, you take for granted that you have a relationship with everything you see. But when the clouds come low and block your vision, the disconnectedness brings insecurity. You know there are things out there, even very close, but because you don't know how close, you're afraid of crashing into them.

I'm not sure how I drove myself to the beach that day. Somehow I arrived safely, and Jessica and I connected. We hugged for a long time, though she did most of the hugging. I just stood there, empty. Broken. Hurting. As a trauma expert and somatic therapist, Jessica helps people to release trauma stored in their nervous system, fascia, and cellular memory. Knowing I was completely stuck in my head fog, she immediately started to help me reconnect with my body.

"Lie back on the sand and feel the earth supporting you. Take some long, deep breaths."

Jess led me through several minutes of breathing and slowly guided me back into my body, gently reminding me to feel each part while encouraging me to notice any tension. She started, "Bring your awareness to the top of your head."

I noticed the tension there and took a breath to both accept and release it if it would loosen. It felt good to breathe. The fog began to lift. I could hear the ocean and feel the breeze at last. I had not felt or heard much of anything for quite some time except the grief, pain, and fear in which I was drowning.

What a gift to listen to Jess's nurturing and powerful voice, metaphorically holding my body and soul at that moment. I surrendered to it, trusting her to guide me through the fog and the waves. I was still sad and afraid; my soul urged me to guard! Protect! Close! It required work to connect, breathe, listen, and feel.

"Now, scan your body and see if you can find Jesus's love."

"It's gone . . . I can't find it." A tear left my right eye, settling uncomfortably in my ear.

She was quiet for a moment. Then intuitively knowing I needed Jesus's love and that it was there for me, she gently urged again, "Find His love, Rena. Where is it?"

Trusting her knowing, I tried again.

"Where are You, Jesus? I need Your love. Where is it?" I pleaded silently.

It took a minute, but there it was, buried deep in my heart, waiting for me to grab hold of it. More tears streamed out as I realized He was there, even though I had so bitterly rejected and cursed Him. He was there loving me compassionately, even though I felt so utterly destroyed and alone.

I'm forever grateful to Jess for giving Jesus back to me. Jessica is not a Christian, but she has challenged and nurtured my relationship with Jesus throughout our twenty-five years of friendship. At this moment, I needed Him more than I ever had. She knew this intuitively and helped me find Him.

Thus began my journey back to Jesus and true freedom. It all started with the revelation of His never-ending love.

Caught in a Rip Tide

The tide changed on Amanda's eighteenth birthday. It had been a wonderful week. We'd celebrated Jeff's parents' fiftieth wedding anniversary in a beautiful cabin in the Northern Sierras with his siblings, their spouses, and our nieces and nephews. Watching the kids hang out with that easy, close friendship unique to cousins was such a joy. Age difference and popularity do not apply to cousins. It's all fun, and each celebrates the other. We had hired a professional photographer to take family photos as a surprise to Jeff's parents, and the photographer also agreed to take senior photos of Amanda. Jeff's sister, Laurie, and I had done a lot of the planning for the family time at the cabin, and it had gone beautifully. I was filled up, satisfied, and tired.

Jeff's brother's family came back to stay in our home for a few more days before returning to Arkansas. The plan was to do a college tour of Pepperdine University with Amanda and her cousin, Shelby, followed by lunch at the beach before taking them to the airport.

I had bought a large, chunky-style Michael Kors watch in gold with rhinestones around the face. I had the gift carefully wrapped and ready to give to Amanda at the beach. The gift was extra special this year because she was turning eighteen. To me, it was a rite of passage for both of us.

I had worked very hard to raise my daughter well. I had given her infinitely more than I had been given emotionally, spiritually, materially . . . really, in every way. I was grateful and satisfied with what I saw in her. She had worked tenaciously, despite her challenging learning disorders and metabolic difficulties. She was an excellent student and a responsible employee and volunteer. She had been baptized the year before. She was a "dream daughter." My dream of a godly family was coming true.

While everyone was getting ready to head out to Pepperdine, Amanda came into our bedroom, saying she needed to talk to us. Her next words completely shattered the dream.

Note to Reader: I know you want to know what she told us. But I really feel it is Amanda's story to tell. I have told my story with all the gory details. That's my prerogative. But I have really told as little as possible about others . . . only where it was absolutely necessary to the overall story. The details of what Amanda told us that day aren't crucial to this overall story. What's important to know is that this was the impetus to my radical freedom journey with Jesus, and what she confessed was a complete mockery of my daily prayer for her that she would always know her worth.

As she told us what happened, I went numb. I began to blame myself. Amanda, knowing I would do that, fiercely scolded me that it was not my fault. I looked around the room, searching for stability, but the room was spinning. The foundation was gone. I had no place to put my feet. It felt like being caught in a riptide—the strong pull of the tide forces you further out against your will as you stretch your toes downward, praying you find the bottom, only to realize even standing is not possible against the power of the tide.

Writing about it now, I still feel the pain and sadness of a lost dream. But at that moment, I could not find my bearings. I could not see the shore or any calmer water, let alone feel or understand my feelings.

Naïvely hoping I could salvage the plan of this dream day, I walked zombie-like through the college tour. All I remember of the tour is standing on some random steps and staring at the ocean. Afterward, I couldn't go to the beach and enjoy lunch with the family. I tried. I pulled myself out of the car and moped toward the sand behind the rest of them. I meant to go. I wanted to put away the pain for later. I wanted to be strong and courageous. But I could not step into the warm softness of the crashing Pacific waves.

Instead, I slumped down, curled up at the low wall that separated the parking lot from the sand, and began to crumble, sobbing uncontrollably. My sister-in-law noticed and came back to comfort me, but there was no consoling me. I just needed to wail and grieve and fall apart. So, that's what I did—

drowning in the deep, churning waters of my broken dreams and emotions.

When they finished lunch, I took my brother-in-law's family to the airport. I was in no state to drive at all, but I couldn't think through my condition, so I stuck to the plan. We were a big group, so we took two cars. Amanda drove home in one car, and I took everyone else to the airport. Driving home alone, the true extent of my devastation hit me. I could not make it the fifty miles home through LA traffic, so I pulled over and called Jessica for help. I hoped she could calm me down enough to get home, at least.

Through sobs, I told her about the revelation of that morning. Jessica listened compassionately, knowing from the sobs and desperation that I was utterly devastated. When she finally spoke beyond, "Oh, honey, I'm so sorry," she said, "So you found out Amanda is pretty ordinary."

What? It wasn't the response I expected, although I knew Jessica would not have the same conservative Christian ideals for her daughter that I had for mine. But it did highlight how much I had hoped and counted on my daughter to be extraordinary. I did not expect her to be perfect . . . no, really, I didn't. But I did expect her to act as if she had great value at her core, and Amanda's revelation had revealed the exact opposite, rocking me right off any foundation I thought I had.

I dropped down into a pit of despair. My faith was gone. I doubted God's existence and spoke hatred against Him . . . *if He was even real.* "I hate a God that would save me but send my daughter to hell!" I cried. I don't mean an eternal damnation hell. I mean hell on earth, like a series of bad life choices that create hell. It felt like my family of origin had just followed me home. It felt like I had fallen into the devil's clutches. And I was an elder's wife. This wasn't good.

Tide Pools and Tidal Waves

Amanda was born on a Saturday afternoon in July. There was a big thunder and lightning storm on the night she was born, which is unusual for Southern California. Having your first child can feel overwhelming, like a tidal wave. But having Amanda felt more like the tide pools that reveal themselves during low tide. It was a sweet time of discovery and wonder. It felt easy and relaxed. We used to play Enya while she napped. Our home was calm.

She was precious! She was an easy baby with strawberry hair and peachy skin. She slept through the night at six weeks. She nursed well for thirteen months. She grew to be very fair with strawberry curls. Her demeanor was sweet and pleasing. My mother-in-law said she had an endearing spirit because her presence made you want to love her and know her more.

Once in school, Amanda began to show signs of learning disorders. This distressed her terribly, and kids teased her because she couldn't learn to read. By the end of second grade, I decided to homeschool her, but she had already decided something was wrong with her. She spent the next ten years working her heart out to keep up with the smartest kids in our community. If you know anything about homeschooling, you know that it can be an elite group.

She managed to hold her own but spent at least four times what the other students invested. She excelled in music, academics, and competitive speech. But I saw the toll it took on her. She cried almost every day, especially as she approached and entered adolescence.

Instead of going with the flow of her gifting, she wanted to face the biggest waves and take them on. Amanda is an artist and a teacher by gifting. Those things are easy for her . . . like super easy. She once copied a Van Gogh painting with finger paints inside of ten minutes when she was eight years old. I didn't even know she was doing it. I did a double-take when I glanced at the kitchen table where she was painting. I framed it, and it still hangs in my house today. I put her in art lessons, and she excelled there too. A couple of years later, she organized a "PE class" for some toddlers in our neighborhood. She brought in five students once a week for two hours and charged two dollars per student.

I watched her run that class with the grace of a seasoned professional. Those kids were mesmerized by her as she taught them about obstacle courses and how to do jumping jacks, read them stories (which she had actually memorized because she still could not read), or seated them in a circle for a snack. I could not have handled five toddlers, and I was thirty-five years old, a mother, and a homeschooler. She had gifts, but she didn't want to pursue those things. "Art is easy," she protested. "I want to do something hard!"

That's another thing about Amanda. She's a hard worker and does not shy away from a challenge. I admire that in her. Things come easier for our boys, but I worried about her least because she knows how to face a challenge.

But when she became involved with boys and then the man she married, she chose challenges. And love and hormones revealed an impulsive, reckless side that we had never seen. She wasn't herself. It was like someone had taken my daughter and put this other person in her place—a person who hated me and Jeff, who wanted to hurt and humiliate us. She looked unstable; it looked like she was falling apart emotionally. Her mood was all over the place. I feared for her welfare because she was so impulsive.

Gone were the days of tide pools.

A Big Set of Waves

So what do you do when the most important dreams of your life are shattered? I mean, once the shock is over and you realize that all you worked for and hoped for might be completely gone?

Jeff went into fix-it mode. Having a mechanical engineering mind, he began to seek solutions. I, on the other hand, cursed God and went to bed. I had no interest in getting out of bed. Why should I? Nothing I did or said had any consequence (hear bitter sarcasm). I was like Mrs. Bennet in *Pride and Prejudice* when Lydia ran away with Mr. Wickham—only quieter. My church family prayed for me. I told them to go ahead if it made them feel better, but I did not think it would help. My entire adult life seemed like a mockery.

I was so angry at God—*if He was even real.* I wanted nothing to do with Him. I was inconsolable and angry, acting just like I had when my mother let me down at age fourteen. It's like when the ocean has no choice against the moon's gravitational pull. Anger pulled at me in an old familiar way. I was protecting myself with anger again, but this time, I was angry at God.

A Different Current

Currents are like highways in the seas, and going against them takes a lot of energy because they are so powerful. We can control the direction of our lives to some degree, but there are currents around us that are out of our control, like someone else's current that collides with our own. Amanda had chosen a different current than the one I had laid out for her. She was heading away from me quickly. I wanted it to be different. But she was choosing.

That day at Santa Claus Beach with Jess was the beginning of my journey to love and transformation. It had nothing to do with Amanda, really. I had a tidal wave reaction to something some people called "ordinary." For whatever reason, this "ordinary" time of a young woman's life was seriously impacting me. Maybe because I sensed that it was not an isolated event. I could feel the current—a powerful highway taking my daughter in a different direction from us. I knew I could not swim against it or pull her out of it. I wanted to, but I knew I was not powerful enough.

I needed to understand that no matter what choices my children make, Jesus is within me, loving me.

With Jess's help that day, I could finally feel Jesus's presence again, and I began a journey to have a relationship with Him. But just as the ocean can be relentless during a swell, this season was relentlessly challenging. Once I made peace with Jesus, I hoped I had learned what I needed to learn and that things would settle down again. But the connection with God was merely the foundation of my lessons. I needed to understand that no matter what choices my children make, Jesus is within me, loving me. I learned to seek and receive a relationship with God even in the scariest, most painful times. These lessons were layered and pulled me into a decidedly new current with Him.

The relationship Amanda had informed us about on her birthday ended, and I hoped the swell was over. But I was wrong. Just six weeks after that day, and two weeks after my day at the beach with Jessica, Amanda told us she was interested in another man she'd met at work. His name was Steven, and he was twenty-five years old. He had a toddler son out of wedlock and was living in a camper shell with no running water or electricity. He had been in gangs and in trouble with the law. He also had a history of a lot of drug abuse.

Are you kidding me? This couldn't be happening. Amanda was barely eighteen years old, a senior in high school, and had just gotten out of a very dysfunctional, if not abusive, relationship. She was in therapy, working toward healing, but here she was, choosing a man who very much resembled my family of origin—the kind of person I'd been running away from all these years. Did she really want to choose this current to swim in? Yes, she did. She jumped in with both feet and swam full speed away from us.

I began to go under again.

Reflections on Living

I love the beach and the ocean. A dip in the ocean is like medicine for the body and soul, but it can also kill. It is a good metaphor for both the perfect times and the most challenging times of life. I have spent many days at the beach saying, "It doesn't get any better than this. This is one of the best moments in life." But I'm not a good swimmer, and I have been caught in a real riptide before and felt the terror and unforgiveness of the ocean. It's good to have a healthy fear of the ocean.

1. Describe a tidal-wave event or season of your life when you felt like you were caught in a riptide and might drown.

_____

_____

_____

_____

_____

_____

2. How did you react or respond to the situation? Did you simply swim horizontally with the beach to get out of the riptide, or did you panic, fight the tide, and almost drown? Tell your story.

_____

_____

_____

_____

_____

3. How did you get to safety again? Who helped rescue you? If you haven't found your way out yet, what do you think you need to do to get to shore?

_____

_____

_____

_____

_____

_____

CHAPTER 10

Steven's House

He called me "Step-avó." He'd coined the name, revealing his sense of humor and his attempt to keep the complexities of his family straight in his head. I was his dad's wife's mother and had given myself the name Avó, which means "grandmother" in Portuguese, when my daughter, his stepmother, had her first son, Hank. Franklin was Steven's son, who was six when he began calling me Half-avó. He explained matter-of-factly that since Hank was his half brother, I must be his Half-avó, thus the name. But when I explained that I was his step-grandmother, like my daughter was his stepmother, he quickly put that together and declared me Step-avó with his crooked smile and twinkling eyes that rarely met another's directly. It was clever, and I preferred it to "Amanda's Mom," which he used to call me before Step-avó.

Whatever the names, we were forging a providential relationship. Amanda sometimes asked me to pick him up from school, and I always said yes if I could swing it. Our after-school ritual was to go to McDonald's. He'd order the spicy McRibs and French fries and would usually devour them before I dropped him at home.

In November 2018, we pulled into the McDonald's drive-thru behind a long line of cars that also needed after-school snacks. A few cars pulled in behind us. It was hot and windy. The day before, the Camp Fire had destroyed hundreds of structures and killed almost a hundred people in Northern California. Even though the Camp Fire was hundreds of miles away, we knew we were having fire weather.

Suddenly, we began to see huge billows of smoke very close to us. Then giant flames appeared way too close to where we were trapped in the drive-thru line. The flames were clearly coming from the property that Steven, Amanda, Franklin, and baby Hank had moved from just two weeks earlier. At first, Franklin was afraid and started to panic. Then he began to cry because he had left some toys in the storage shed next to his old house. He was sure they were being destroyed.

I scanned the immediate area for fire fuel and hazards, reassuring Franklin that we were safe. We were right next door to a gas station, but there was no brush near us, and the roofs were tile. I told myself we were safe, but that line could not move quickly enough for me. Then a huge commercial plane flew terribly low overhead, dropping a massive load of pink fire retardant. We could see it landing on cars in a nearby parking lot, and Franklin laughed. It was a nice tension reliever, but we could still see giant flames whipping in the wind and heading too quickly into our town—right on top of Franklin's recently vacated home.

The home sat on a property that seemed out of place in our middle-class suburban town. It feels like you've been transported into a third-world-type neighborhood. There's a small home, a few shed-like dwellings, and an old camper shell. The lone camper shell that sits in a larger separated portion of the property was where Steven had been living when he met our daughter in September 2013, shortly after she turned eighteen. The outside of it appeared old, dirty, and dilapidated. I can't describe it well because I've only seen it from the outside and never close up, but I know it had no running water or electricity.

A year after we met Steven, he moved into one of the shed-like dwellings that I called "the shack." The shack was basically in the backyard of the one legitimate home on the property. It had one sink in the kitchenette area and a tiny room with a stall shower and toilet. You could smell the mold in the walls and see the tiles were cracking and broken because the floor was not sound. The ceiling was slanted and did not look stable. It was barely livable . . . third-worldish. Eventually, my daughter, their newborn son, Hank, and Franklin lived there together.

The fire did burn the one house there to the ground, exposing the metal piping typically hidden in the walls, attic, and foundation. The dense smoke descended with lightning speed. The heat was so intense that it broke out windows and melted the door to the shack. Providentially, my daughter and her little family had moved to a small apartment less than two weeks before the fire. Had they still lived there, Amanda would likely have been inside the shack with Hank, then sixteen months old, who would have been napping, which is why she had asked me to pick up Franklin that day.

If you've never lived through a California wildfire, it's hard to imagine just how fast the Santa Ana winds can whip up a fire. Ten minutes before the house was engulfed in flames, there was no sign of fire. *Suddenly* is not a good enough word. Thank God they were not in the shack that day.

The House That Built Me

Maybe it was the fleas that attacked my ankles from our stained carpets in the summertime. Or the thick cigarette smoke that smacked me in the face every time I walked through the front door. I was embarrassed about the ugly, old, mismatched furniture. Of course, I could never have friends over for sleepovers because of the pot smoking and my papa's drunken visits. No one ever said so explicitly. I just knew, in the way all children in alcoholic families know. It was one of many unspoken family rules.

Miranda Lambert has a song called "The House That Built Me." It's a smart title because of the play on words. The song tells the story of a woman who has lost her way in the world. She goes back to her childhood home to remember who she is. We usually think of building a house. Yet it is so true that the house we grow up in plays a role in building us into who we become.

My first home was chaotic and embarrassing. Later, it was dangerous and demonic. That home built insecurity, shame, codependency, fear, anger, and sadness inside my little soul. I was full of broken-down walls and a foundation with a deep, cavernous hole. I knew that home was not livable, but I had no idea how to build a sound home. Still, I knew staying was not safe, so I left that home as soon as possible.

Home can be a place that builds a good foundation in you, a place you want to return to when you lose your way, that reminds you of who you are and what you knew before you lost your way or got beat up by the cruel world. Or it can be a place that leaves you in pieces, like the sticks and stones I saw in Moore, Oklahoma, after the tornado hit. It can leave you looking more like an abandoned construction site, left behind due to a lack of funds or capable contractors. Not done and not done right. It can feel like you need to tear the whole thing down and start over from the foundation.

One of Jeff's mottos, when he makes a mistake building something is, "It's faster the second time." While that is true, it does take a significant amount of time and effort to rebuild a house from the foundation to the roof. That's what I had to do. I wanted a home with security, stability, warmth, and beauty for my children. I hoped it would be a house that built them well.

The little I had learned about Steven's home growing up sounded an awful lot like mine.

Steven's Family Home

When Amanda began to date Steven, her now husband, I was freaked out. I knew he carried many of the familiar spirits that oppressed my family. The chains I had tried to break, the walls I had tried to build to protect my daughter—they were failing me completely. Before I even met Steven, I knew he was essentially homeless, living in a camper shell with no running water or electricity. I knew he was in his mid-twenties and had a toddler son out of wedlock. I knew he'd been into drugs and in gangs. I didn't need to know anymore. He was not the one for my daughter.

I think Amanda wanted to do this right, so she had him come to Jeff and ask permission to date her. Jeff said no. Still, she wanted me to meet him too, so we set up a time for him to come to our house. When he stepped through my front door and hugged my daughter, the hair stood up on the back of my neck, and my stomach dropped. I almost puked right there. It's like a part of me recognized him because of my upbringing. He was like all the men I'd grown up around who'd scared me.

I sat Steven down and started asking him questions about his life. He was clearly trying to be winsome and humble, but it wasn't working. As far as I was concerned, he had nothing to recommend himself. I learned he had no men in his life who supported him or who he respected. He told me his father was a falling-down drunk and that he had learned to drive at twelve because his father was too drunk to drive. He said his grandfather was not speaking to him. When I asked why, he blamed his grandfather, saying the grandfather was crazy and needed someone to be angry at.

That may have been true, but I judged Steven as having no self-evaluation skills or a sense of personal responsibility. He communicated that his life situation was the fault of others, a victim of circumstances. He did have a job working steadily as a plumber. That was fine, but I could see every one of those red flags waving in front of me. I was not convinced in any way.

I told him a little about me and then wished him well. I told him he wasn't as far along on his journey to making a life for himself as I had hoped, and until he was, he was not in a right place to date our very young daughter.

I could also see my daughter was utterly naïve to the ramifications of a relationship with him, and she saw me only as judgmental. She was right about that part. My fear was ruling my reaction, and I was judging him hard.

Besides, she was barely eighteen and a senior in high school, so I thought I had a say. That turned out to be a wrong assumption. Amanda was mad at me. I guess I had given him the third degree and then rejected him, and that wasn't fair. Of course I rejected him! Wouldn't you have done the same?

Jeff could see some attributes in Steven that Amanda was attracted to. He also felt responsible for being loving to a person who needed guidance and community. Steven started attending our church, and we began walking a tightrope between being good Christian people and protecting our daughter. We wanted to be loving and kind, but we didn't want him to think we approved of him for Amanda.

And then, during a family therapy session with Jeff, Amanda, and me, she told us that she was in love with Steven, and they wanted to get married. The therapist talked about life stages and how Amanda was still in high school, and this guy had essentially been married and had children. She tried to convince Amanda that because she was at least two life stages behind Steven, it wasn't a good idea to be making commitments to him. Before the session ended, Amanda was almost hysterical. She left and didn't come home; she wouldn't answer our calls. She had never done anything like this before. We were sick and scared.

My memory is cloudy here, but eventually, she came home by the next morning, but she'd decided she would no longer listen to us. We ended up having one of those "if you're going to live here, you need to honor our rules" talks. She said she would move out. We took her phone away, and Steven bought her a new one. She dropped all of her classes at the community college . . . I'm not sure why. It wasn't consequential because she had already fulfilled her high school requirements, but we were concerned that she would do that without even having a conversation with us.

Meanwhile, Amanda had earned a very good scholarship to Colorado Christian University (CCU), and we were thrilled for her. Plus, we had family friends who lived near there. They had a one-year-old and a finished studio in their basement and were looking for someone to help with their son. Jeff thought moving her out there would be a good idea. He hoped she could make a new life near her university and get away from Steven and her fights with us. I hoped so too. We called them and told them all the gory details, and they said they would love to have her. I drove her out there, set her up in the little apartment, and drove away.

To be honest, I did not even miss her for the first month. It was such a relief to be free from all the tension, arguing, and stress of what she would do next with Steven. I felt weird and guilty about that, but it's the truth. People kept asking if I missed her, assuming I must miss her so much. And I did—I was missing my little girl—the young woman I hoped she would be. I was missing the relationship I wanted with my daughter.

I was grieving, but it wasn't for the person I had dropped off in Colorado.

Steven continued to go to our church and sit near us. With Amanda far away, we could more easily connect with him. We began to pour into him a bit. Not because we wanted to but because Holy Spirit was telling us to. Jeff went through a book with him and our son, Nick, about dating. We took him to see a movie about Noah's Ark and then went to coffee and talked about it. I continued to pray for him.

In that brief time of getting to know Steven, he had barely shown me the front door of the home where he had come of age. But I could see inside the entire place. I knew my daughter had absolutely no concept of what I saw . . . mainly because we had given her a home completely free from such dangers. I could feel her resistance to my opinions, and I felt helpless to make her understand. Still, I had to try.

I continued to warn her about the dangers of his home. I told her that there were likely abusive perpetrators in his family. I didn't assume this as a judgment against Steven or his family. I simply knew because I had lived in the same type of home. I worried constantly. Intrusive, fearful thoughts plagued me all day long. I prayed like the desperate mother that I was.

Housing the Holy Spirit

Our bodies are temples of the Holy Spirit who is in us (1 Corinthians 6:19). Some people call that still small voice *intuition or deep knowing*. Some people use those words to do whatever their ego or fleshly will desires. But if we are honest and humble and ask, we can access the wisdom and power of the Holy Spirit because He does dwell in us. We are not just flesh and blood. Most of the time, we need that deep wisdom to navigate life—especially when going through difficult transitions like childhood to adulthood.

Amanda needed Holy Spirit. And He spoke clearly to her at times. Before she moved to Colorado, she woke from a nightmare in the middle of the night. She felt a demonic presence crushing her. She came into our room crying and asking for prayer, so we prayed over her. We could feel the darkness lifting and an angelic presence hovering. Her breathing slowed, and she stopped crying. I asked her what she was thinking.

"I think I should go to CCU and study the Bible," she said.

"Sounds like a word from the Lord," I replied.

Then she began to cry, saying, "But I don't want to study the Bible because I can't get a job with that."

We smiled affectionately because that was such an Amanda thing to say. Historically, she had always been so responsible and planned carefully for her future. This was our Amanda. It wasn't the reckless, unpredictable, rebellious eighteen-year-old. Still, her comment revealed a lack of trust and fear about the future. We encouraged her to listen to what she hears from Holy Spirit in these moments of clarity and walk in faith. We assured her that God had something higher in mind by telling her to study the Bible.

She moved away from the idea within a couple of weeks, and when I reminded her of what she had heard from Holy Spirit, she became annoyed and put me off. I just prayed quietly.

When we went to CCU's orientation week, they had a worship service when all the new students were gathered for the first time. Before each song, they read a chapter of the book of Ephesians. It just so happened that Amanda had been reading the same book in her daily quiet meditation time. She heard clearly during that worship set that she was in the right place and that God was with her. She'd had doubts throughout that summer, and she was still struggling with being away from home and away from Steven, but Holy Spirit gave her clear assurance, and she knew it enough to tell me.

Throughout that year, several painfully disappointing things occurred in their relationship. I don't want to list every event, partly because I don't need to make a case for my pain or worry and because it would be straight gossip. Suffice it to say that I had spent that year emotionally and spiritually on the floor, bleeding out. It wasn't all bad, as I will discuss at length in the final section of this book. But it was intense and impossibly difficult.

God often speaks clearly to Amanda; it's a real gift. Back then, though, she did not follow through with the clear instruction, counsel, and revelation the Holy Spirit gave to her.

We had a front-row seat to a spiritual battle waging within our daughter. She would break up with Steven but then be angry with Jeff and me. She would be convicted in her spirit, apologize to us, and tell us she was like rebellious Israel. Honestly, I had whiplash from the back and forth. I could not get my bearings. But her ups and downs with Steven were not because we pleaded with her. I think they were because of what she heard in her quiet times with Jesus.

One day, we were on vacation in Alabama when Jeff got a phone call from Amanda. She admitted to him that her entire relationship with Steven was sin and darkness. She told him that she was done with it. She had been planning to go with Steven to meet his family in Seattle, and she was still going to do that, but when they got back, she was calling it quits. Her mentors and community had already advised her not to go, but she was unmoved. Jeff gently talked to her and listened. While in Seattle, Steven proposed, and she said, "Yes." I cried.

She assured us that she would finish school before getting married, but instead, after only a year of college, Steven flew to Colorado, packed her up, and drove her back to California to live in his shack without discussing anything with us.

Followed Home

The next three years were CRAZY! It was a wild roller coaster ride that seemed to be going steeply down most of the time. How could there be so much plummeting? As my husband tried to salvage the situation and restore hope for my daughter, she continued to slip through our fingers. Every good effort seemed to explode in our faces, and good intentions seemed to get twisted into something malignant. We were losing her all at once and bit by bit. We missed her. We feared for her. I was gripped by fear often.

We could see she needed something from us, but we couldn't figure out what. Or what she seemed to need, we found impossible to give. It was the saddest time of our lives. We held each other and grieved hard throughout that season.

So, as I prayed constantly, hopeful things would happen; God was answering my pleas. Amanda would hear something from the Lord and tell us about it. But just as soon as we felt hopeful that the situation was being redeemed, another painful decision would play out before us. Unless you were in my closest inner circle, and I talked to you every day, which was like . . . two people, I didn't want to talk about it. People would ask how things were going with Amanda, but there was no way to give an answer that would even scratch the surface. Too many deep and wide and huge things transpired every week. How could I let someone in by answering a question like that when I hadn't talked to them in a month or two? It was impossible. The roller coaster was intense, and we were on it alone.

I don't even want to write about this time. My whole body feels sick. My body is remembering the trauma, the sadness, the grief, the fear, the humiliation, the anger, the hatred, the rejection, and the pain. Jeff and I held each other and cried and grieved so often. We looked into each other's eyes and knew we were feeling exactly the same. No one else on earth could understand, but we understood each other completely. It was utter helplessness, utter grief. We missed her so badly that our souls were bleeding to death.

Maybe it felt like how Jesus may have felt when His people rejected Him. There He was, God, taking on human form to show how much He loved us, conquering death and the demonic through the sacrificial death and the pouring out of His blood. And yet, the very ones He loved so much and was rescuing were driving nails into His hands and feet and pounding the cross into the ground while mocking Him. Without being blasphemous, in some small but profound way, we related to Jesus.

Breaking free from painful generational patterns doesn't happen by kicking people out of your life.

When Amanda was twenty years old, she married Steven in a little chapel in Las Vegas. They moved into the shack together, and she began step-mothering Franklin. Before their first anniversary, she was pregnant. She gave birth to Henry Travis Lewis "Hank" just eleven days before she turned twenty-one. At that moment, our family and Steven's family became one.

So Steven's house came to my home. Steven's home of chaos, poverty, promiscuity, abuse, broken families, incest, drug addiction, and criminal incarceration came into my sweet, safe home that I had built and guarded so carefully. Steven's house, which was terrifyingly reminiscent of my own family of origin's house, had followed me home.

Despite hours and hours of prayers on my face daily, begging God to kick Steven out of my family, He was showing me that His ways are higher. Breaking free from painful generational patterns doesn't happen by kicking people out of your life. But without a wholly shattered heart, the Lord could not convince me of this truth.

Reflections on Living

I was very determined to create a different kind of home from which I came. I was sure of what it should look like. So, through the years, Jeff and I developed and orchestrated the Roberts home. It did not come naturally to me. I was intentional and thoughtful and worked the plan diligently and vigilantly. I wonder if you have given the idea much thought. Take a minute now to reflect.

1. What was the house that built you like?

_____

_____

_____

_____

2. What aspects have you changed? Or what aspects do you plan to change?

_____

_____

_____

_____

3. Which of those things that you wanted to change, if any, have followed you home? Which aspects do you most fear will follow you home?

_____

_____

_____

_____

Carol, who helped me get into Pepperdine University, and me (26).

Grandpa Sidwell, my father's father, who was notified by the sheriff's department when I got caught stealing. He was the one who loaned me money to get to Pepperdine and tore up the promissory note when I graduated.

Me (19) and Jeff, on our first date. See my bad hair day?

My stepdad (Daddy)   Me (22)   My dad

At my Pepperdine Graduation

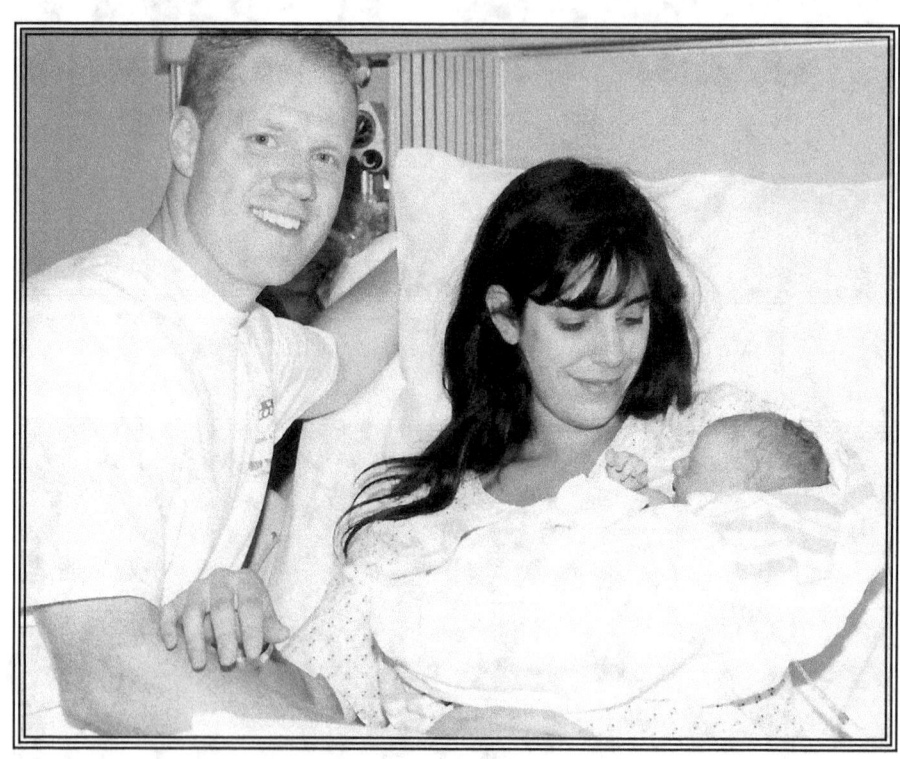

Jeff and I with Amanda the moment she was born in 1995.

PART THREE

Loving

CHAPTER 11

Free to Love

*E*very good story must be staged. The best stories don't start at the beginning. There are usually countless details of circumstance and character development before you are introduced to the story. Often, the first several chapters of a good book set the stage. You may even think you're reading the story when, in fact, the real story has not even begun yet. I'm always so impressed at how fiction authors can weave the back story into their books seamlessly and at just the right time. I love that moment in reading a book when I say out loud, "Oohhh, now it all makes sense."

So far, I have been setting the stage for how to walk in supernatural Love that brings true freedom despite our family patterns, generational curses, and dark pasts. In case the sequence of events has gotten confusing for you, as I was confused while living through some of this life, I will spell it out more simply here.

Act One

There I was, living my life to the best of my ability. I had done as much right as I possibly could. I was focused on being sure Amanda was ready for college. She was my oldest child, and I felt a solemn responsibility to be sure she would have all she needed and to give her the absolute best opportunity possible to be successful in life.

This was diametrically opposed to all that I lacked at her age. When I was eighteen, my mother was a crack addict, and my father didn't help me apply for college or support me financially in any way. I was alone and afraid for my future.

Sure, there were times when Amanda was "bratty" about my planning, but I just chalked it up to adolescence. I really felt she was just immature and would thank me later. We were family. We had created a beautiful family together. Every day, I was there for her, dedicated to her and the rest of the family. Her father and I had a good marriage. We modeled respect and cared for each other and our family. We were a good family. I thought we would be loyal to each other despite our imperfections.

Act Two

This is why Amanda's apparent rebellion so blindsided me. It devastated me on so many levels. My parents had hurt me; my husband had hurt me; friends had hurt me. But Amanda's action cut me to the core. It felt deeply personal. Nothing I had experienced before compared to this pain of rejection by a treasured child to whom I had dedicated every moment of my life since her birth. The sleepless nights, the prayer, the worry, the action, the work, and the financial investment—I had done it all with pleasure and joy. How could she reject me?

I understand rationally now that she was trying to become her own self, differentiated from her family of origin. This is a normal part of growing up. Unfortunately, that separation can be painful. My mother-in-law nailed it when she said, "That mother-daughter separation can be bloody." Indeed, I was bleeding on the floor. I had no idea how to move forward and no motivation to get up. Why should I? My most important life project had utterly failed.

Yes, that's the second piece. First, I was personally hurt. Second, I experienced her rebellion as my own failure. Honestly, I could not wrap my head around how my efforts could have failed. I could not have tried harder. Even as I think about it now, all I can think of to describe my disillusionment is a cartoon caricature. I see that moment when the character looks at the audience and springs pop out of its head in every direction while its eyes morph into spirals turning opposite directions.

How could my plan and its execution have produced such hostility and rejection?

Act Three

The third piece was the spiritual blow. I'm sure my spiritual breakdown was a reaction to or a product of my personal response relationally and internally to the situation. If I hadn't been so personally wounded and if I hadn't internalized the situation as an existential failure, my spiritual condition would not have plummeted so completely. But I was wrecked in my soul and flesh, resulting in a total spiritual breakdown. My relationship with God went directly into the toilet. I literally doubted the existence of God. I felt my whole life had been in vain. If indeed God existed, I hated Him because He had allowed my daughter to make terrible decisions despite everything I had invested in her. I specifically doubted the reality of God and His goodness.

I was angrier with God than I have ever been with anyone else in my entire life.

So there I was in the worst emotional pain of my life, and I had no God. When I was younger, and the adults in my life were letting me down, I knew God cared. When I was an adolescent and making tragic choices of my own, I knew God still loved me, forgave me, and was for me no matter what. But when my daughter made choices that mocked my daily prayer for her—"May she always know her value, that she is worthy of love"—it seemed I knew nothing about God. When I thought God had let me down, I lost my foundation. I was free-falling, and it was not good.

And this was all before Amanda even met Steven. Before things really went south, in my estimation.

It wasn't until my friend Jessica helped me reconnect with Jesus that day on Santa Claus Beach (see chapter 9), that I began to find hope again. I tried to see how I had contributed to Amanda's decision-making. I repented. I figured her mistake was a hiccup and that we would get back on track.

And then Amanda met Steven. By that time, we didn't trust her to make good decisions because she had made so many poor decisions just a month before she met him. Plus, he did not meet the requirements of a person I would ever allow to spend time alone with any of my children, let alone carry a romantic interest in my daughter. And yet, somewhere inside, I knew that I would not be able to stop it.

Thankfully, I had my Jesus anew, and He was my only hope. For the first time in my adult life, I had nothing else I could put my hope in because, in addition to the effect it was having on our family, the situation was negatively impacting long-term friendships and our church community. So many aspects of stability in our lives were shaken and stripped away.

The Stage Is Set

This is the stage God set to begin writing the story of a new me. Old sets, props, and storylines—used, played out, and left untidy—littered the dark corners of the stage. You couldn't really see them anymore except in your memory. The spotlight was on me now. I appeared to be all alone. I surely felt alone. It was time for the final act.

When Amanda was three, she asked me, "Mommy, do you know who is with you when you're alone?"

"No, honey, who?"

"God and your shadow."

There I stood alone on the stage—me, God, and my shadow. I was about to dive deep into all three. And with just those, God would give me a hands-on master's level degree in Love, knowing that freedom was required first—the freedom to love unconditionally.

The rest of this book chronicles that process—my journey to freedom. It was grueling and exhilarating. Daily struggles with humiliation and disappointment were mixed with moments of great joy and deep faith. Precepts of Christianity that I had long heard, believed, and talked about became qualitatively and distinctly real as never before. My attempt to narrate this process may be clumsy at times, but I know Holy Spirit will give you precisely what you need this day from my sharing. He is good that way if you ask and are open to receiving.

Breaking Free to Freedom

They say the truth will set you free. Jesus said that. He said, "And you shall know the truth and the truth shall make you free" (John 8:32 NKJV). He also said, "I am the way, the truth, and the life. No one comes to the Father except through Me" (John 14:6 NKJV). Of course, I agree with Jesus. In addition, and importantly, I believe "Loving" shall make you free. Or maybe Jesus enables us to Love supernaturally, and walking in that Love is the perfect description of freedom. Better yet, maybe freedom means we are free to pour the supernatural Love of God out on everyone, everywhere we go.

Freedom means walking through life on earth by the Spirit and not the flesh, which is only achievable by walking very closely with God.

I've titled this final section Loving because I know that Loving is both the *catalyst* and the *result* of breaking free from every dark generational pattern in existence. I'm talking about the painful generational patterns of my family of origin and your family of origin. Indeed, I'm talking about the deep generational pain of the entire human race. This is what Holy Spirit told me to write down for you. I believe this message is to encourage and instruct, and I pray I am successful in these goals.

What I mean by freedom is freedom from many things. Freedom from self. Freedom from habitual sin and character problems. It could be "big" sins, like chronic drunkenness (alcoholism) or adultery. It could just as easily and more likely be freedom from a critical spirit that speaks negatively of others and self. Freedom can be a total mind and perspective shift, so you are free to see things from a heavenly perspective. Freedom can mean setting boundaries in relationships and breaking free from codependent familial ties.

Ultimately, freedom means walking through life on earth by the Spirit and not the flesh, which is only achievable by walking very closely with God.

So, how does one become free? Can freedom come all at once? Of course it can. Jesus freed the demoniac in an instant so that he went from literally crazy, dwelling among the tombs in chains one minute, to walking around town in his right mind the very next (Luke 8:26–39). Freedom can also come bit by bit as you give yourself over more and more to God, as the Bible talks about us going from glory to glory. I have experienced freedom in both ways. But more often, freedom comes more like a circle . . . but not a perfect circle. It's circular—up, down, and back around with no apparent order.

Because the prominent tenets of Christianity seem to layer in and through and on top of and below each other, it's impossible to have one without the others. This fact and realization have made it difficult to decide where to start. Should I lay the foundation and begin with brokenness or intimacy? Or should I begin with forgiveness and repentance? And, of course, there's Love and Mercy and Grace. This is why this section on Loving has been so tricky both to live and write for you.

I experienced a total transformation of self that happened dynamically, sometimes while I was lying on the spiritual operating table, half-dead, needing to die completely. But how do I explain a process I am still engaged in? I can't tell you everything about it until I get through it myself, right?

I can't, but if I stop trying in my own strength and trust the Spirit to flow through me, He will give you exactly what you need on your freedom journey.

Do What the Bible Says—Obedience

On my journey to freedom, I was convicted to the core of a simple truth that many Christians often do not heed—the word of God is serious. God means what He says and expects obedience. God's Word is not to be used to control others; it's to be applied to our hearts, minds, and actions. For real! Phrases like "nobody's perfect" don't fly with God.

Now, I don't mean legalism or merciless judgment if you do not obey. I don't mean to judge you or anyone else. However, as adopted sons and daughters of the God of heaven and earth, we are to walk in the power of His Holy Spirit that He gave to us. It's not just a good idea; it's a lifestyle that we must walk out. You will see the term "walk out" throughout this section. In order to become a truly loving human, you must walk out Jesus's principles, and that requires obedience.

This truth about God's Word became more and more apparent to me as

I thought about how I was chronically frustrated with the church because I didn't see the claims of Christ actually happening, and I definitely was not free. As I was being set free—experiencing real tangible change within me— things I could never accomplish by my own will and power—Holy Spirit began to drill into me how serious He is about His Word. Read the following Scriptures aloud. Are they true or not? Will you live like they are true, or will you make an excuse?

He has shown you, O mortal, what is good. And what
does the LORD require of you? To *act justly* and to
love mercy and to *walk humbly with your God*.
(Micah 6:8 emphasis mine)

You have heard that it was said, "Love your neighbor and hate your enemy."
But I tell you, *love your enemies and pray for those who persecute you,*
(Matthew 5:43–45 emphasis mine)

But *seek first* his kingdom and his righteousness,
(Matthew 6:33 emphasis mine)

And when you stand praying, if you hold anything
against anyone, *forgive* them,
(Mark 11:25 emphasis mine)

These verses of the Bible are not shown in their context. However, I can assure you that none of them include a caveat such as: "Unless someone steals your daughter," "Unless someone lies to you and manipulates you," "Unless someone gossips about you or spreads lies about you," or even "Unless you are completely in the right according to Scripture." There are no caveats.

The Bible clearly states, and Jesus demonstrated, that we are to love everybody all the time. We don't really love at all if we only do it when it feels good. That's not much more than acting loving because we want to. I'm not saying that treating someone nicely or in a loving manner can't bless them or that it's not good. I'm saying that is not the type of love the Bible is talking about, and it is not the kind of love Christ demonstrated.

So, what does it mean to truly love our enemies? It does not mean just saying we do. Heidi Baker, founder and CEO of Iris Global, a ministry that serves the poor, destitute, lost, and forgotten people across the globe, often says, "Love looks like something." She is right. And, oh, the death of self that occurs when we allow the Holy Spirit to change our hearts and then walk out that change. Because you see, Holy Spirit can soften our hearts and give us supernatural love for someone, but if we don't walk that out, our hearts will turn to stone again.

I had to begin with lordship issues, which is where I will start in the next chapter. By rooting out the idolatry in my life, I began a new journey of faith. I am in no way saying that it is the only beginning point. The Lord is so personal and deals with each of us individually. This is my story. You have your own, and I encourage you to pursue it in the perfect way for you.

To take hold of freedom, there are some basic and crucial practices and principles that one must walk out. The following Scriptures describe what it means to walk out obedience.

———

Resist the devil, and he will flee from you.
(James 4:7)

———

We demolish arguments and every pretension that sets
itself up against the knowledge of God, and we take captive
every thought to make it obedient to Christ.
(2 Corinthians 10:5)

———

"Get behind me, Satan," he [Jesus] said. "You do not have in
mind the concerns of God, but merely human concerns."
(Mark 8:33)

———

We cannot simply agree with these principles or even pray fervently through these and for these ideas. We must *do* them.

Barbara prayed over me, taught me to pray, and always pointed me to listen to Holy Spirit. Those encounters were miraculous in and of themselves.

I was blown away by hearing clear, godly wisdom when asking and listening in prayer to Holy Spirit. But no change occurred in me until I actually walked out (obeyed) the truths that Holy Spirit revealed to me in those moments.

No change will occur until we walk out the truths that Holy Spirit reveals to us.

Witnessing the transformation in me, friends and family have asked how I found such freedom. Some have seen that I no longer worry. I honestly have peace and freedom from fear. That was not the case for me for most of my life. Others have seen the supernatural Love I now carry. They say they want it too. But getting there is a process, and that's what I want to show you.

Walk Out Your Transformation

The walk out is part of the fun because it means Holy Spirit is strengthening and cementing the work He has begun in you. The enemy is afraid of the person you might become and the power of God that might come through you. And the walk out is a large part of an intimate walk with Jesus. It's what He does in you and what you do with Him. That's fun, no matter how difficult it may seem. Admittedly, some of it isn't fun at the moment. But in retrospect and with the right perspective, it can indeed be fun at the moment.

Transformation happens in the heart. Jesus talks about this in Matthew 13 when He uses the analogy (parable) of the seeds and the soil they fell upon. What is the soil of your heart like? We can know what's in our hearts by what we think about and focus on. To receive the seeds the Holy Spirit wants to sow in us, we must prepare the soil of our hearts.

Each of the following chapters will challenge you to examine your heart and take action to create a beautiful garden therein. You may have to pull weeds, get rid of bad soil, add in new, rich soil containing all the necessary nutrients, plant good seeds, and tend to it every day. Our hearts are big and complicated. They need daily attention to remain free from darkness.

This final section of *Long Live Love: Walking Out Freedom from Painful Generational Patterns* attempts to outline for you the main tenets and daily details I applied as I broke free. As you may expect, breaking free does not include changing others. But it may change and definitely impact everyone around you, including your family and posterity. It offers them a model and an invitation. But the change, as always, starts with you. By walking this way, you break free. I am free! I have discovered that real transformation is possible. Totally possible. You can have that. I have found that. I have fought for that. I have pursued it wholeheartedly, and it is a reality!

Reflections on Loving

Transformation is challenging to the flesh, but nothing is better than the freedom to love supernaturally. Let's get specific about breaking free.

1. What are you most desiring to be free from?

_____

_____

_____

_____

2. What does freedom look like to you?

_____

_____

_____

_____

3. What worries you most about letting go of your ways and allowing God to transform you?

_____

_____

_____

_____

_____

CHAPTER 12

Lordship

Sobbing into the phone, I blurted out to Barbara what had become apparent, hoping she would have a magical solution. I recounted every detail while snot dripped into my mouth. Maybe she knew some special Holy Spirit prayer that would cause Amanda to repent and be eternally safe from bad decisions. My brother-in-law said this would be just part of our family's testimony. Screw that! I did not want a testimony. I already had a testimony. Goodness gracious, isn't the story of my life enough of a testimony to the power and Love of God? No! I was counting on Barbara to make it stop somehow. She listened quietly, holding the cathartic space I desperately needed.

"My children are my whole, wide world!"

And that's where Barbara broke into my self-pity. "Okay, Rena. Now I understand why you are so devastated."

Oh, how good it feels to be validated. She understood how hard I had tried. She understood how much God had let me down. She understood how important it was that we fix this. She understood. And then she said it.

"Your children are a lord in your life. You need to repent for idolatry."

I gasped incredulously, stunned into silence. What did she mean I needed to repent? How could she say that? I had dedicated my children to Jesus from birth. I'd read the Bible to them every day. I did everything possible to point them to Christ. I strategized, made clear plans, and then I worked to carry out those plans every day, praying for help where I fell short. Why was I the one who needed to repent?

But I didn't say any of that because I knew she was right.

God's ways are so impossible for us. How could I have loved my children so fiercely, worked so steadfastly to raise them in "the way they should go" (Proverbs 22:6), and not make them an idol in my life? It's so tricky because I was pouring faith and Bible all over them, but I was utterly deceived into thinking I had prioritized God over all.

I had no idea until that very moment that my children had become my idols. I'd thought Jesus was my Lord. But my family was.

Lordship Isn't Cool

Most of what I will write about in this section will seem brave and virtuous. Forgiveness, humility, and love are impressive to most anyone—Christian, agnostic, or even the staunchest atheist. But lordship is not universally accepted as a good thing. In fact, many in our society would call it ignorance or even mental instability. So why start here? I guess because that is where God starts. It was the first command He gave to the Jewish people. He said, "I am the LORD your God, who brought you out of the land of Egypt, out of the house of slavery. You shall have no other gods before me" (Exodus 20:2–3).

It all starts with God. We think it begins with us. We are so tempted to start with ourselves. But it's the wrong premise, and we end up in pain and fear and disappointment every time we start with ourselves.

In my case, I had been delivered from my family-of-origin patterns on many levels. My brother, for example, had been abused and lived a life that landed him in prison multiple times. I'm the only person in my bloodline who has stayed married and raised an intact family. I was able to get free from abusive situations and not repeat them in my adult life for my children to witness and suffer that trauma. So He really is "the LORD my God who brought me out of . . . the house of slavery" (Exodus 20:2).

Lordship is where Barb began with me. Living in this world of flesh and blood and matter, it's natural to put things on earth before God—like a house remodel, the opinions of others, church, career, community, and money. I knew this command well. Seeking to live outside of the natural realm and desiring to live supernaturally, I regularly took stock of myself to see what I was putting before God in my life, and I intentionally readjusted my priorities in tangible ways.

At this moment of crisis, though, Barbara helped me see that I had put my children and family before God. I felt tricked! All the dedication and work I had given to my children was for the purpose of raising them for God. I found a journal entry from 2010. My children were nine, twelve, and fifteen at the time I wrote it:

9-13-10

The First Day of School

Oh Lord, please help us today. I do not know what to do. I do not know how to handle all these problems.[14] Please, Lord, help my children learn. Help them grow in You. Help me be prudent in my anger and an example of the things I try to teach . . . Help me, Lord, to be an encourager. Help me encourage and not allow them to debunk it. Help me to be wise and clever.

I love you, Lord.

Thank you for hearing my prayers.

This journal entry of a homeschool mom making goals and establishing a school year in prayer certainly doesn't exactly seem idolatrous. It shows my heart and desires to serve God and to be a good servant and mother. That's tricky, though, because two things can be true simultaneously. I can love God but love my children more. I did. You probably do, too, if you're normal and honest.

It's so hard for these flesh-and-blood bodies we live in to see beyond the material world. Especially in the western world, where we have countless material possessions, tools, and products to improve and preserve our lives. The Bible says, "For where your treasure is, there your heart will be also" (Matthew 6:21). We treasure our children and our families. We spend all we have on them. And therefore, our hearts stay here on earth with them.

That's what I did. The Bible says to "seek first his kingdom" (Matthew 6:33), and that command is closely tied to Exodus 20:3—to have no other gods before Him.

First things first . . . who or what is your god? Who or what do you put first in your life? I was putting my children and my husband first. And when I realized this, I repented.

> I use my will to declare and align myself, my actions, thoughts, and values to the will of God, which is to have no other gods before Him.

Repentance Is Cool

Since I will be repenting a lot throughout this last section, I invite you to do the same. That said, it's only appropriate to expand on the idea of repentance. The word *repentance* is translated from the Greek word *metanoia*. In trying to translate this word into English literally, scholars landed on "to think differently afterward" or "changing your mind after being with."[15] After being with God and hearing from Holy Spirit, I am often moved to repentance. I like this definition of repentance, taken from an article published on gentlechristian-parenting.com:

> Biblical repentance means responding to God's love by being transformed in your convictions and actions. It means turning towards God and away from whatever dishonors Him. Biblical repentance is not about your emotions, your sin, your efforts, or your resolve. It's about your surrender.[16]

How I reestablished God as Lord of my life was simple. It took an act of my will, which may seem paradoxical because, ultimately, my will needs to be put to death. But God loves paradox, so both are true. I use my will to declare and align myself, my actions, thoughts, and values to the will of God, which is to have no other gods before Him.

So that day, with fresh revelation that I had allowed my family to become my idol, I declared to the Lord—out loud with Barbara leading me—these words:

> *"Jesus, I repent for my idolatry. I repent for making my children gods in my life. I repent for making my husband and my home gods in my life. I choose this day to place them and hold them in their proper place."*

Then I added the most important declaration, although both are necessary:

> *"Jesus, I receive you as my only Lord and Master. I seek to follow You and You alone."*

Awareness and Intention Are Powerful

It had been a difficult year, and I needed some space to rest, heal, and rejuvenate. (That in itself is a concept many of us don't consider. I'm just now learning that it's beneficial, if not essential.) Anyway, I went away for four days by myself. I stayed at a nice hotel and spa near my home. I planned to meditate daily on something heavenly.

The first morning, I decided to meditate on Jesus. As I set that intention, I quickly realized I could not connect with Jesus. I felt distracted, tense, and anxious. I began to pray for my children and their specific problems, none of which were small, mundane issues. I sensed a difficulty in trusting Jesus to help with these things I had been praying for months and even years.

As I noticed all of this and continued to breathe in and out with intention, Holy Spirit showed me that I was seeking *help* instead of seeking *Jesus*. There it was. Again and still, I wanted Jesus to help my children *more* than I wanted Jesus.

It's a subtle difference. Praying for others, especially our children, is good. The Bible tells us to pray for each other. Praying fervently for my children as they maneuver young adulthood and life's challenges is not wrong. But I had my children on the throne. I was looking at them first.

As I write this, I realize how stupid that is because focusing on them causes anxiety.

Consequences of Idolatry

As I continued in meditation, Holy Spirit revealed what I think is a spiritual consequence of idolatry. I began to see in the Spirit a cancerous black ball of fear on my right side near my heart area. It was below my collarbone but above my breast. It looked like a piece of an asteroid or lava rock. I knew in my spirit that it was a fear cancer, and I needed it removed, but I did not know how to get rid of it. Then I became aware of how I fed it all day long. I won't belabor it, but Holy Spirit showed me how I ordered my days around trying to help fix all these problems I was praying for. And, of course, I could not fix any of them. No wonder I was anxious.

A lifestyle of idolatry is disappointing and carries dark consequences. When I saw that fear cancer in my chest, I also felt the force of the demonic because the fear felt like a type of bondage. I was somehow chained to this thing that was hurting me. The cancer was blocking me from the divine flowing of the love and peace of God. Instead, I was anxious and tense.

Even though this example is a nuanced picture of idolatry, I knew I was seeking my children's well-being above Jesus. And I was working to help them, serving them as my little gods rather than seeking and serving Jesus first.

A few weeks later, still battling this cancer, I was at church praying earnestly for my child during the set of worship that followed the sermon. I begged God to make him well. Suddenly, I felt Jesus take my chin and gently raise it so our eyes could meet. I didn't see Him visually, but in the Spirit, I connected with Him. The message was clear, "You want your son to be safe more than you want Me."

I nodded in agreement, knowing that was exactly what was keeping me sick with the fear cancer.

"As long as you seek your children's well-being first, you will be afraid," He continued.

I prayed aloud while the music continued. "I repent for making my children's well-being a lord in my life. Jesus, You are my only Lord and Master."

Instantaneously, I remembered how He had told me that He has my children. I remembered how I had practiced giving Amanda to God every hour. I realized it was time for a refresher course to give my children to God, to trust Him with their well-being, and seek His kingdom first. I remembered that I already knew I really had no real control over my adult children's lives. I already knew that worry and control are fruitless gods. And just then, a bit of the black turned to light. There was still the walk out of this prayer moment. Honestly, I'm in the middle of that now. Walking it out day by day, moment by moment, allowing my falls to teach me to get a little more cancer-free every day.

Ironically, my children are better off when I have things in better order. At the very least, their mama is not hosting a fear cancer in her chest. That's gotta be good for something, right? Beyond that, though, I can bring Jesus more readily. I don't talk about Jesus or tell them about Jesus or teach them about how the answers to their life problems can be resolved through a relationship with Jesus or by following the Bible, or by adopting a Christian worldview. Those are good things, of course, but my days of training and teaching my children are over. Instead, I carry the presence of God with me, bringing it into every relationship and circumstance, and that changes the environment profoundly. And my children are watching and are keenly sensing my energy and motivations.

In a way, I'm right back where I started. It's that circular nature of freedom I talked about in chapter 11. We don't achieve freedom in a specific area and never deal with it again. There's always a new, deeper lesson. Each time we walk out that level of freedom, we become freer. It's a process. I am in the process. It's a pursuit of the heavenly over the flesh. Today, I choose God over the little gods of the earth.

Reflections on Loving

If you are ready to choose Jesus over the little gods in your life, don't delay. Go ahead and say this prayer, filling in the blanks of whatever you are idolizing.

Pray, "Holy Spirit, show me what other gods I have before You."

Wait . . . listen . . . now write them down. It could be one thing or twenty things.

_____

_____

_____

_____

_____

_____

_____

Now pray, "Jesus, I repent for allowing anything to become a god in my life before You."

Referring to the list you wrote above, speak each item, one at a time, repeating the phrase, "I repent for making [x] a god in my life."

Finish your prayer with, "I choose to place all of these little gods in their proper place. Jesus, I receive You as my only Lord and Master. I seek to follow You alone. Amen."

CHAPTER 13

Intimacy

Everything happens in intimate engagement with God. Literally, every-thing in this final section flows out of intimacy. Repentance happens. Forgiveness happens. Faith expounds. Miracles abound. Joy is real. Gratitude grows. Fear flees. Freedom reigns.

Have you ever had a friend who calls you up to higher things? They call when you need to hear the truth rather than for someone to tickle your ears. Intimacy with God is like that, times infinity. There is no end to how engag-ing intimately with the Lord transforms you. So, in all subsequent chapters, understand that spending time and being close to Jesus is paramount because it transforms our hearts and brings true sonship identity to us as His children. Jesus implores us to be in Him and promises He will be in us. That's pretty close. He tells us in John 15:4, "Remain in me, as I also remain in you. No branch can bear fruit by itself; it must remain in the vine. Neither can you bear fruit unless you remain in me."

In March 2016, the night before Amanda married Steven, I could not sleep. Around two in the morning, I went downstairs to the swimming pool courtyard and parked myself on a lounge chair. With worship music playing on my phone, I cried and prayed and worshipped. The song lyrics were my only words at first as I sang about how the glory of God's presence puts my soul at rest, fills me with peace, and integrates my joy and pain into a whole, beautiful person.

I had prayed for months for God to keep Amanda from marrying Steven. I begged Him for hours every day for their relationship to end. I was praying for her future and the generations to follow. Simultaneously, I had been walking out the most intense transformative sanctification process of my life. I was so grateful for the freedom Jesus had gifted me thus far. And I was sure He was going to answer my prayer.

I guess I thought all of that intimacy with the Lord meant He should give me the desires of my heart. Doesn't the Bible say that the prayer of a righteous man accomplishes much (James 5:16)? Doesn't it also say that He will give us whatever we want if we ask by faith (Mark 11:24)? Put simply, I had been standing in faith that God would answer my prayers and stop a lifelong connection between Steven and Amanda before it ever got started. So there I was, the night before, wondering how God would stop this wedding.

During that time down at the pool, however, the Lord showed me how small my faith really was. He showed me how hurt I had been that He hadn't answered my prayers. He showed me my ugly heart. I knew He was right, so I began to pray earnestly for a new heart. I told Him I was sorry for not seeing His eternal plan and repented for looking only at what I see here on earth. I asked for more faith, and He gave me peace. I found myself praising Him as the righteous One, the One who is Joy, Peace, and Love, over and over. His presence filled me, and I was well. In Jesus's name, walls of bitterness broke down. They were gone. I love Jesus.

I couldn't feel His Love when I first went down to the pool, so I doubted it because of what was happening in the natural. How could He love me and allow this? I felt let down, forsaken . . . as if He didn't love me. I realized this and confessed it as a lie, saying, "I repent for believing the lie that You do not love me, God." Holy Spirit revealed to my spirit the truth that God truly does love me so much. He allows trials as an invitation to intimacy to bring me closer and become more dependent on Him simply because He wants me and loves me. I could see, then, that His goal was not even to use my life. Instead, I was to stay low. He whispered to my heart, "Stay low, humble. Be humble."

Stay low, humble. Be humble.

As I worshipped and allowed Holy Spirit to take control of my thoughts, prayers, and proclamations, my entire agenda began to shift. Instead of *my will be done,* I prayed *Your will be done* and begged Him to bring Kingdom Love down here to the earth. I said, "I love You, Jesus. I love Your presence." That's when I felt His peace. I was no longer afraid. I went forth in confidence as I surrendered all to Jesus.

When I reflect on how this all took place, I recall praying this way: "Holy Spirit, I trust You with Amanda. You Love her. You made her so loving and compassionate. I am sorry that I have hurt her. Help me bless her today. I love You, Jesus. Holy Spirit, fill me up. Fill me. Break my heart and give me a new one."

It worked; my prayer was effective, but I had to continue in praise and prayer, or the pain and fear would return. So I kept crying out to the Father, "Good and Gracious God, hold me close. I cannot do it without you. You're my only hope. I don't care what anyone thinks. I love You."

Plus, if I didn't stay in a posture of submissive prayer, the fear of losing my own hopes and dreams for the future would torture me. So, I kept at it, "I must cling to You today. You're my only hope. You're all I have, Lord. I need You desperately. I give all pain to You. I give dreams and hopes to You. I love You. I give it to You. I can't fathom what You've given."

I continued to trade my will for the will of God as I prayed. "Please bless Amanda and Steven in Jesus's name. Please bless them. No matter what, I choose to pray for Your will to be done. Thank You for Your perfect will, Jesus. I don't care what they think."

Notice how I kept returning to the words, "I don't care what they think"? Holy Spirit had revealed that I was partnering with pride and fear of man. So

I quickly repented for pride and fear of man, which are both lordship issues. It's so crazy how every intimate interaction with Jesus is thoroughly cleansing and connecting and convicting all simultaneously.

In the spirit of Philippians 3:10, I prayed one last prayer. "I give my reputation to You. Thank You for killing me. Let me die. Let me conform to Your death." This, after two years of begging for this day not to happen. It was, without a doubt, a supernatural shift.

Seeking Intimacy with God

If I can't hear from the Lord, I'm doomed to struggle and be miserable. To get through the hardest times in life, I need closeness with God the Father, the Son, and the Holy Spirit. If I don't have that, it's like losing the dearest person to me and trying to be comforted by strangers. Their comfort is kind and not totally meaningless, but I need my best friend, lover, children, favorite aunt—the people closest to me who know me. The people I know who know me, see me, and care for me. But these days, all those people feel like strangers compared to God because I have learned how to be close to Him.

Getting close to God was hard at first. It was awkward and often felt fruitless. Sometimes I couldn't feel His presence at all. Sometimes it was vague, and I wasn't sure what He was communicating. And sometimes His presence surrounded me entirely and spoke clear, supernatural words and ideas of healing and Kingdom. At first, I wasn't sure I could be really close to God. I read books about it and watched YouTube videos of people teaching on the topic. I knew Jesus was close to the Father because He said, "I and the Father are one" (John 10:30) and, "the Father is in me, and I in the Father" (John 10:38). That sounds really close. I knew I did not have that, and I was pretty lost and miserable. That's when I began a journey of closeness with God.

I watched a lot of Heidi Baker's YouTube videos. If you have watched her, you know her teaching style is to worship and then tell stories or testify as to what God has done and what He's teaching her through her ministry. That's it. She does not prepare teachings. When I first began watching her, she looked so strange to me. She would get on stage and usually sit or lay on the floor and begin to worship God as if she were alone. Over and over, she would chant things like, "We love You, Jesus," "We glorify Your Name," "We praise You, Father God," and "We want more of You, Jesus."

But she knew she wasn't alone because, in between her declarations of love for God, she would encourage the audience. "Tell Him you love Him, tell Him you want more of Him," for example. Her body rocked, and her arms waved as she continued in an almost incomprehensible conversation with God. Honestly, I thought she was weird, and I knew my husband would discount her completely as a wacko or something, but still . . .

There is a difference between flesh and spirit. The Bible says to worship in spirit and truth. It does not say to worship in the flesh. I get the idea that worship often means transcending the flesh and moving into the spirit realm because God is Spirit. As I watched Heidi Baker, I recognized that my flesh was offended. Her style bothered my sense of etiquette. It went against the traditions of the churches I had attended regularly.

However, I learned that just because a certain way of engaging God offended my flesh, it did not mean it was wrong or even weird. In both Heidi and my cousin, Barbara, I saw relationships with God marked by the fruits of the Spirit, which are love, joy, peace, patience, goodness, kindness, faithfulness, gentleness, and self-control (Galatians 5:22–23). I saw the supernatural fruit of healing and deliverance working within and through them and those they touched. I wanted that.

I knew somehow that if I wanted true intimacy with God, I might have to look a little strange too. I went for it. At first, it was clumsy and didn't really work, but I kept going because, well, I needed God for real. His statutes weren't enough. His Word wasn't enough. His community (church body) wasn't enough. Only He was able to satisfy my grief, fear, and general lostness. I knew that instinctively, so I began my journey to Jesus.

I pursued intimacy specifically and as a matter of practice. At first, I started with ten minutes of my quiet time set aside for intimacy. Sometimes, I would just focus on God, maybe slowly repeating, "Be still, and know that I am God" (Psalm 46:10). Sometimes, I would listen to "soaking" music—slow, worshipful music with lyrics about closeness with God. I found recordings online where someone read Scripture about God's love for us while meditative music played in the background. I soaked in these meditative selections.

If something was pressing on my heart, I brought it to God. Usually, I asked, "Holy Spirit, what do you say about [this situation]? I want to hear from You. I want Your ideas." Other times, I simply sat quietly and asked, "Holy

Spirit, what should I do today?" However I tried, the intention was always the same. I set the intention each day to grow more closely intimate with God.

Another way I built intimacy with God was by asking Him about pretty much everything. You know those people who, whenever you ask them to do something, say they will pray about it? Those people used to annoy me. "Really?" I thought. "You gotta pray about whether or not you will go to a birthday party?" You know the Scripture that says not to judge because the very way you judge, that judgment will come upon you? (Matthew 7:1–2) Uh, yeah, that's me.

I've learned intimacy with God builds
sensitivity to the Spirit.

I know we have freedom in Christ and can do whatever we want. I know God is not offended if I go to this or that party. I don't think He's like that at all. I don't think He sees one perfect order for each of our days, and we are either on that path, or we're doing the wrong thing. Not at all. I believe God is far more dynamic and freer and enjoys the process of our freedom. I also think He enjoys showing off by making good and even wonderful things happen out of our total fails. But that's another topic.

Nevertheless, I began bringing even the smallest decisions and thoughts before the Lord. If I had a negative thought about a situation, I would quietly pray, "Holy Spirit is that from You for wisdom or a warning? Is it a critical spirit within me that I need to take captive and kick out?" And then I'd listen expectantly, testing the answer against the Bible and the fruits of the Spirit. If I sensed a warning, it would be confirmed by nudging or instruction bathed in compassion, humility, and grace. If it was a critical spirit, I might notice my thoughts wandering to past offenses or justifications for the negative thought. See the difference?

I've learned that intimacy with God builds sensitivity to the Spirit. It's such a sweet and peaceful place to be. Every intimate moment is unique. I could liken it to spending time with a close friend. You never know exactly how the conversation will go, but you will communicate, and a good friend will make you better and nurture more fondness between the two of you. Sometimes, she will point out where you are off track and help you see the higher path.

When I move into intimacy through prayer, the prayer shifts to a conversation where I am mostly quiet, except I begin to pray the words of the Spirit. It's like my will conforms to His will, and my eyes start to focus through His lenses. My prayer shifts from my supplications to His truths and His destiny for myself and whatever situation or person I am praying for. Then I am no longer conformed to this world but transformed by the renewing of my mind as the Spirit pours His thoughts and ideas into my mind (Romans 12:2).

Through this daily practice of focusing inward and upward and listening, I learned to hear His voice that truly is within each of us. This is what Jesus meant when He said to remain in Him, and He will remain in us (John 15:4). If we slow down enough and set the intention to listen and act on *His voice* rather than all the other noise, we can connect with the knowing God gives us and live by the security that comes from intimacy with Holy Spirit.

The Fruit of Intimacy

In her book *Birthing the Miraculous,* Heidi Baker says, "There are no shortcuts to the anointing. If we want to fully walk out the callings the Lord places on our lives, we must spend time with Him, cultivating intimacy."[17] Heidi's ministry has seen—no joke—bona fide blind, gray, clouded eyes turn dark brown and see! The entire premise of her book is that the miraculous comes through intimacy with Jesus. We may be able to experience miraculous things at times, but to live from a place of transformation, freedom, love, and even miracles, we must have intimacy with Christ.

On January 1, 2019, I settled down to spend time with Holy Spirit. As I've said, this process is harder than others because my mind wants to wander. But this particular morning, I was immediately taken into a vision which is pretty rare but very cool.

I was on a sort of spaceship, sitting in Jesus's lap, looking out at the cosmos. It was reminiscent of Princess Leia in her last movie *Star Wars: The Last Jedi,* right before she died. I knew there was a battle waging outside, but I had a protective shield, like the force field in *Star Wars;* it was all around where I was sitting with Jesus. It extended very far out into the cosmos. I could barely see in the distance that angels were battling on my behalf, which was great. But the shield was absolutely impenetrable. I was so keenly aware of its strength that the enemy's efforts were laughable; I began to laugh out loud.

So there I was, lying on my living room sofa at 4:30 in the morning, spending time with the Lord, and laughing loudly and jubilantly at the enemy trying to destroy me. The enemy's efforts were utterly in vain. In my mind, I felt the Lord revealing clearly that worry and fear of the enemy's schemes were completely unnecessary. I knew that Scripture in Romans 8:31, "What, then, shall we say in response to these things? If God is for us, who can be against us?" was truer than truth itself. There was no need to focus on any evidence on the earth that might point to the victory of darkness. As clearly as I knew my eyes were brown, I was protected and safe. There could be no convincing me otherwise. Wow, this was awesome! I began to pray for more. "Lord," I said, "Make the shield bigger. Make it cover my entire house, children, husband, loved ones, and whole earth!" Why not? It was such a lavish gift. Why not ask for more?

When I got up from the sofa, I was literally drunk in the Spirit. I bumped into the fireplace mantle and the island in my kitchen as I made my way through my house. It took about thirty minutes to recover from that time with the Lord. It was a sweet recovery, and the rest of the day was joyful and peaceful. I was grateful for that gift.

The next morning, I again sat down to experience and hear from the Lord. This time, I felt nudged to give some love to the homeless people I would encounter the next day in Hollywood. My family had planned to see a musical at the Pantages Theater, and apparently, the Lord wanted to let some homeless people know that He loved them and that they weren't forgotten. I wasn't sure how I might be used for this. So I prayed this prayer:

> *Lord, show me what to bring to homeless people. Prepare me to pray for the homeless because homeless, mentally ill, and drug-addicted people scare me. Thank You, Jesus, that You love all. Help me resonate with Your Love and send out a powerful frequency of Your Love. I see Your shield of protection around me. I do not need to be afraid. Thank You. You are Love.*

The Holy Spirit immediately answered me and helped me pray. Soon, I was praying in the Spirit. Here is that simple, beautiful prayer:

Lord, Your destiny for them. You care about them. Your destiny upon them! May they turn to You and repent zealously and receive You into their hearts to change them and heal them completely. Thank You, Lord.

I decided to make some nice soup because it was particularly cold that week. Feeling unsure how to convey the message I felt the Lord wanted me to convey, I thought I would just offer the warm homemade butternut curry ginger soup to some people in Jesus's name. I intended to look for an opportunity to pray for anyone who would let me. But when the time came, I didn't see as many homeless people as I usually do on Hollywood Boulevard. I found a few and gave them the soup, but none were open to prayer or any type of connection.

As I went into the theater, I thought, "Oh well. A least I was obedient and tried, in my feeble way, to offer the Love of God to those few people." Still, I wondered if I had missed something or if God's plan had been thwarted in some way because I had failed to hear clearly from Him.

The show was incredible. I love musicals and always have. After taking pictures in front of the theater to commemorate the special occasion, we headed back to our car. My sons were on either side of me when a man came toward us, yelling obscenities at me and calling me obscene names.

He pointed at me aggressively, saying, "You're a piece of s*#@! You're a b*#@#!!" Normally, this would have upset me. I would've felt threatened and hurt. I'm a super sensitive, girly type of person, and naturally, colorful characters in cities at night make me uneasy. But this night, it was different. Supernaturally, I was calm and unmoved by his aggressive behavior. I simply looked into his eyes, completely sans fear. As he passed me, I turned and kept looking at him. He looked back at me, then turned around to come back toward me, continuing to assault me verbally.

I saw my youngest son's hand go up in front of the man's face to keep him away. Still, I was unaffected by his ugliness toward me. Instead, I began to speak. "It's okay," I said. "I know, I love you." I repeated this softly as he hurried back toward me with his finger pointing right at me. The second he entered my sphere, his entire demeanor transformed. He began to cry and apologize and told me I was beautiful.

Somehow, this did not surprise me at all, and I continued to repeat that it was okay and that I loved him. He began to confess, saying that he had envy in his heart and he was a jealous person. I repeated the words, "It's okay. I know. I love you," like a gentle chant or mantra. Then he began to spill his pain, telling me that his husband had left him that day, and he was brokenhearted. The next thing I knew, I was embracing this man and holding his pain. At this point, I began responding to his repeated professions of my beauty by saying it was Jesus who was beautiful and Jesus who loved him. And we began to dialogue about that.

"Do you really believe in God?" he asked.

"Absolutely," I replied. "God is here now.

"So, you really believe in God for real?"

"Yes! This is God here. Not me. I don't do this. He loves you and is using me to show you that."

Sobbing, the man pleaded, "Please, don't ever leave me!"

"Jesus is here, and He will never leave you. He wants you to know that."

"I want to go home with you and live with you forever," the man replied.

"Your home is with Jesus, and you can be with Him forever. Pray to Him."

He circled back to, "So, you really believe in God?"

"Yes," I answered. "He's here now."

It went on from there in between sobs and hugs. It was the most bizarre and beautiful thing I have ever experienced. The man was dirty and stinky and very likely out of his mind. Maybe he was just high on something. Our meeting began with him verbally assaulting me and coming at me in a physically aggressive manner. Yet there I was, hugging, holding, and speaking life and truth to him.

Whether he was or not, I can tell you I was definitely out of *my* mind. Rena's mind would've fled the scene as soon as possible and never looked back. But through seeking intimacy with God, I had received the mind of Christ (1 Corinthians 2:16) and the heart of the Father for the lost. I was given the wild privilege of embodying them in full color.

After that, I was flying high emotionally and spiritually. I couldn't shut up about it while driving home. I kept wanting to retell parts of the story so the others who had witnessed it could assure me it really happened. My poor son had experienced such a rush of adrenaline, thinking he would have to take this guy down. He could not calm down for over an hour. He wanted me to shut up about it. It was an intense and powerful experience.

Looking back at that prayer, which I am so glad I had written down, I'm so set on fire by the Goodness of God to answer my prayer so immediately. *Immediately,* He showed me how to pray for the homeless people I would meet. I wasn't to pray that they would get off drugs or look more respectable or even start going to church. I was to pray for them to live out God's destiny for their lives and to be healed by receiving Jesus into their hearts.

And my prayer to resonate with Holy Love was clearly evident that night. I was sending out a powerful frequency of Love that caused zealous repentance in that man. I think about how he would pull away from our embrace and say, "Do you really believe in God? For real? He's really real to you?" I am sure he knows the source of that love and received the message I gave him to pursue it more. This just encourages me to believe this man is well today. Wow! I believe by faith that man is full of Jesus today and well on his way to a life of Love and Freedom. I'd love to run into him again.

I want more of those experiences. I want to live a life full of happenings like that. I know it came out of my pursuing God for deeper intimacy with Him. He was living in me, which impacted the world wherever I had contact. That was some sweet fruit.

> *Oh, Lord, thank You for that experience. Thank You for filling me up more and more. I invite You in deeper and deeper. I love You, Jesus, Father, and Holy Spirit. Thank You, Lord. You are good and worthy of all praise and worship forever and ever and ever. Amen.*

Needing Intimacy from Others Less

As I continued seeking intimacy with God, I noticed I began to need others less. My whole life had been a series of disappointments from other humans. I think what happened with my daughter was so painful to me in part because I assumed we would always be close and care for each other. Her separation and lack of care for our family unit during that season were unthinkable and gut-wrenching to me. I do not pretend to think that I am unique in this at all. Indeed, I know I have been hurtful and disappointing to everyone I've been close to. Probably and especially to my husband and children. But I have always loved people and wanted intimacy with them. I had a friend "break up" with me once. She was my best friend. I loved her dearly, and we were very close. Then one day, she started blowing me off. When I pressed her about it, she said I wanted more "intimacy" than she did in a friendship and didn't want to be close to me anymore. I was devastated. But it shows that I tend to seek deep, intimate relationships with people. I guess I sort of required it.

As I began to seek intimacy with Jesus, that need for intimacy with others shifted completely. I really don't feel a need for people anymore. Of course, I love my family and friends. We are close and spend a lot of time together. Ironically, as I need them less, they come to me more and share more intimately with me. A friend of mine often says, "God winked at me." This is one of those winks. As I've grown closer to God, I've grown closer to people; they disappoint me less, and I hope I disappoint them less. Now I long for alone time to have my Jesus time. Even as I've been writing this, I stopped for a bit and put my hands on my heart, which I often do when I'm engaging with God, and bent myself over, rocking and breathing in a moment with my Father. I miss Him when I'm not spending time with Him. He's truly my best friend, my perfect Father, and my supernatural guide. I love Him.

Walking Out Intimacy

Within a month of the event detailed above, I had an interaction with my family of origin that felt like that old familiar lying codependent-denial garbage. The details of what happened aren't important. What is important is that my immediate reaction was to judge and reject them. I didn't know what to feel or think. As if I can tell myself what to feel. I'm a therapist. I actually know better than that. But sometimes, it would be nice to tell myself what to feel.

I knew to pray, though, so I prayed for healing and restoration. I prayed for the truth to be revealed. I prayed for light to illuminate the dark areas of the situation. Can you sense the judgment and my will in these prayers? I prayed for repentance for judging and assuming the worst. I prayed to walk out my faith by Loving them all supernaturally.

But to be honest, I was floundering. I didn't necessarily feel like loving them. I felt like a victim of their dysfunction and found myself judging them and reliving how they had lied to me and hurt me in the past. Why on earth would I believe them now? I wanted to cut them out of my heart completely. But I also knew this wasn't the freedom and supernatural Love God had given me, so I felt guilty and sad.

If I pressed into the Lord, I knew He would restore me, and it would happen in His perfect timing. Maybe I would flounder just long enough to keep me humble or remind me of something that I needed reminding of. I did not know everything; I just knew He would restore me. Here's what that looked like.

The situation with my family occurred on a Monday. On that same Friday, I began my regular quiet time, which I have most mornings from four to five. I pictured Jacob's ladder and a door open in heaven (Genesis 28:10–15). In my imagination and by faith, I climbed this ladder. I saw Jesus standing there, inviting me to walk through the door into heaven. I started to walk in, but intuitively, I knew I needed to have some things cleaned out of my heart before I entered heaven.

I began to search myself, or rather, I allowed Jesus to search my heart for any old, fleshly parts of myself that I had taken back or that still needed to be offered to Him. Ahhh, there it was. I saw my judgment and asked Jesus to take it. The spirit of offense was hanging out in my heart, and I told Jesus I was sorry. I asked Him to remove it. Again. I became aware of self-righteous pride and repented quickly, knowing Jesus is the only Right and Righteous One. Pride is almost laughable in the presence of the Lord.

"I don't know why I keep picking this up," I said. "Please forgive me and remove all pride from my heart." I took deep breaths, exhaling as I let it go. This first part happened very quickly, and a rush of peace and forgiveness and Love filled my heart. And I felt Jesus invite me into heaven.

I told Him I wanted to fly, so we flew around, and He showed me my house. On the way there, He ministered to my heart. I hadn't realized that I'd been feeling guilty and wondering if I was wrong for keeping thick boundaries with my family of origin. Jesus spoke to my heart, saying, "You have a separate path from your family." I immediately began to cry. Not because I was sad to walk separately, but because He saw the guilt I was feeling and assuaged it with those words. Jesus is so sweet that way. He sees every part. But then

He addressed the pride and judgment that sometimes arise in me by saying, "Yours may be a parallel path (meaning they may be walking with the Lord too), but it is separate."

When we finally arrived at my heavenly house, it was clear that it was my house. It didn't belong to my children or my husband at all. It was all mine. Lately, I'd been fantasizing about a larger closet. I have a decent-sized closet, but all my husband's shoes are in it, and he's started putting some clothes in it, too. I know he doesn't have room in his own closet for his shoes. So instead of having them strewn around the room, hall, and bathroom, I gave up my shoe area for him. I knew the bedroom didn't have enough closet space when we built it . . . see how far this goes back? I want a nice walk-in closet with a place for everything, and only my things are there. I'd been thinking about how I could move some walls in our house and create a space for me.

So when Jesus took me to my house in heaven, we went straight to the closet. It was huge and bright! I'm not even sure if it was contained within walls. It was really big. And then He began to show me its contents. There were no clothes or shoes or belts or hats or jewelry safes. Instead, there were people's hearts hanging. Not gross like in a cannibalistic way, but the hearts I hold dear, the hearts I will bless, and the hearts I need to bless more—they were all displayed for me to admire and love. Literally, I could go into my closet, find a heart, and bestow more love on it. Jesus showed me all the hearts I have collected and that He has given me to minister to. Maybe I need to shop for more hearts to put into my heavenly closet instead of shoes!

There were also entire mountain ranges—the Sierra Nevadas were definitely there in my closet—and rivers and deserts and tropical beaches. That closet contained all the places I valued on earth as beautiful manifestations of God's majesty. They were the places that stirred up gratitude, praise, and reflection on the goodness of God within me.

There was also beautiful artwork displayed perfectly for me to enjoy. The artwork seemed to represent how we partner with God's creative power to display His beauty. I'm no artist. I cannot draw a good circle. But artists do create remarkable testimonies as they embody the creative image of God through their lives and their work. There were praises and prayers and words from God everywhere. This was some closet.

All of this, I could see from the door. What if I went inside? I think He was showing me what treasure is and what I treasure. Thank You, Jesus. I came out of that encounter filled to the brim with His Love and Goodness, totally free of all that family-of-origin junk I had been battling all week long. Yay, God!

This is a wonderful story, but don't miss that the walk out required humility, repentance, and waiting.

God's Love and Intimacy

Pursuing intimacy with God helps us to love a little more as He loves—whether we want to or not. The Bible says that "God is love" (1 John 4:8). I can hardly fathom what that means. It's for sure beyond me. But when I study Jesus, I see He ministered to the socially unaccepted, unclean, and revolting, including prostitutes, lepers, and even tax collectors, who were especially reviled by the Jews (Luke 5:30–32). Even during His ultimate suffering on the cross, Jesus gave loving attention to the criminal next to Him, extending mercy and, indeed, salvation (Luke 23:39–43). Even more, the Bible calls this man a "thief," but the original language and what we know about capital punishment in ancient Rome imply he must have been a violent man who battered and even murdered his victims.[18] So, how could God save someone like that? I thought He was just? But God does not show partiality when it comes to His love. He can't help but love each and every one of us—it's His essence.

When I'm faced with "bad" people who hurt me, intimacy with God moves me to love that person for real, just as He loves that person. Understand it's not a love I can just conjure on my own. My flesh is repelled by that person, but God's Spirit softens my heart supernaturally and helps me see them in a new light—how God sees them. We may not love murderers and thieves and the dredges of society, but God does because He desires redemption for everyone. He sees what they can become, not where they are now. And we shouldn't be surprised that He asks us to do the same.

I'm so grateful that all of my children are alive and well. That is no small blessing. There were times when I felt I was losing my daughter completely. I felt her future was being murdered. I even feared that physical abuse could cause her physical death. To be clear, I now know my son-in-law is not physically abusive to my daughter, but that was my fear at one point. As I detailed earlier, I know what domestic abuse is firsthand, so the idea of my daughter being abused in the future and possibly even murdered gripped me with fear.

Maybe you think this is too dramatic. Nevertheless, you'd better believe I was crying out to God to save my daughter from this situation. I prayed this prayer all day long because I saw the attachment as a threat to her future. Worry consumed me every waking hour, so I had plenty of opportunities to practice taking every thought captive (2 Corinthians 10:5). It haunted me in my dreams, so I prayed without ceasing (1 Thessalonians 5:17) for God to get her out of this situation. The worry led to awful narratives in my head of that worst-case scenario. Those thoughts led to anger and hatred of Steven. I literally began asking God to take his life if necessary. I tried to bargain with God, promising to take care of Steven's son if he could just get into a really bad car accident and not be able to marry my daughter. Can we say, "murder in my heart?" (1 John 3:15) Yes. I was committing murder. But check out what God did.

As I was praying to get rid of Steven in any way possible, Holy Spirit took hold of my prayer, and I found myself praying blessing on Steven. Not just, "Oh God, please bless Steven." No, I began praying specific, powerful, chain-breaking, generational-curse-breaking blessings. I'd be wandering around my backyard, crying out for my daughter, and the next thing I knew, I'd be praying for God's kingdom to come into Steven's life, for him to be free of tormenting spirits of pain and child abuse.

Holy Spirit gave me Spirit-filled words of life and destiny for Steven. I began to declare him a forerunner in his family to break generational curses and to bring freedom and deliverance to his entire family. Holy Spirit gently enlightened me that this man was just like me, or I was just like him. I wanted better for my children, and so did Steven. I prayed these prayers aloud in my library, in my backyard, in my car, or wherever I happened to be when the Spirit began praying through me. I knew the prayers were God's will and destiny for this man. I knew God loves us all no matter what, and God knew this man and his family needed prayer. But even as I prayed, I admit I was thinking, *Really, God? Really?*

"Yes, really, Rena."

The Love Identity of Intimacy

Even in that intense, surrendered place, I am aware of my self-seeking nature. Drawing near means I see my unworthiness to be close to God. I'm aware of my unholiness. I'm particularly aware of my sins, again, specifically. This deep knowing of the truth of my depravity ushers immediate repentance from my heart. My heart is to repent now! There is no urge to defend myself or explain my position on any matter. There is no excuse for any thought or action I am participating in. The only real and right thing is perfect Love, which, of course, I know I fall short of, so I repent quickly.

Intimacy with God reminds me of who I am and beckons me to walk in that identity.

But there is no condemnation. I don't even think I experience any guilt or shame. I just know I fall short, and exactly how. This Love shows me my sin. This Love is what propels me to repent fearlessly. Then it rushes in and fills me to the extent that I acknowledge and repent for sin. I say it fills me completely because it does. This experience has happened to me several times, and I can see I am giving up some of myself, little by little. God fills me by degrees. Or maybe there is just always more Love. I know He knows what He's doing. To me, it feels like I am being completely filled with supernatural Love. That is how I experience intimacy with God.

Even as I use words like "repent," "sin," and "depravity," I'm aware that they fall short. I think it's more like I am shown the truth about me and how far I have wandered from my truest identity—the "me" that is united with Christ, one with God and God's nature. That is who I am. I am created in the image of God, yet so often, I act as though I do not enjoy that divine identity. But intimacy with God reminds me of who I am and beckons me to walk in that identity.

It also transforms my heart and mind. There is no way I cannot be changed by it. When I somehow miraculously come into the presence of God while lying on my back lawn, for example, and I become keenly aware of my depravity, repent immediately, and God's Love rushes into every cell of my being, I have no choice but to be changed. The biggest change is humility mixed with forgiveness, compassion, and *understanding*.

When I experience God seeing my depravity, I feel no judgment from Him. There truly is no condemnation from Him. In a moment, I am humbled and see whomever I had been previously judging or whomever I have ever judged completely different. I see how I am just like them. I see how much God loves them. I understand the God-part of their heart. I guess it's the image of God in them that I can clearly see. I almost don't need to forgive them because I stop holding onto offense. But I do forgive them from my heart. I'm also not afraid of being hurt by anyone. It no longer matters because I know, know, know that God loves me, and that is all I need to walk without fear.

Intimacy, then, fills me with His Love, which transforms my heart and mind and allows me to give supernatural Love to everyone freely. I can give Love to my worst enemy and the scary-looking drug addict on the street. I think one reason my actions become so fearless is that the things of this world grow dim. I begin to know that the spiritual realm is more real than the natural realm. Even my husband and children have become less important. I only need God and His Love, and I need Him desperately.

Paradoxically, this perspective propels me to love more fully and fearlessly the people of the natural realm.

Writing this makes me want to stop writing and spend the rest of the day with Holy Spirit! But I know I need to write because that's the other thing that happens as I dwell with the Lord. He shows me things and tells me things He is doing in my life and what He wants me to do. He wants me to testify of the power and joy of intimacy with Him because He wants this with you. *All of you*. I hope many of you read this and know how much God Loves you and how much He desires to change you into His image through intimacy.

I encourage you to explore a deeper intimacy with the Lord and allow Him to lead you perfectly in that process for you.

Reflections on Loving

Paul's prayer for the church in Ephesus two thousand years ago invites intimacy with God through Christ (Ephesians 3:14–19 MSG). I encourage you to read the verses below slowly, taking a deep breath after each sentence.

Meditate on it. Before you start, set the intention in your mind and heart to draw intimately close to God. Your will is powerful, so just intending to do it is very powerful. Here we go.

"My response is to get down on my knees before the Father."

(deep breath; maybe get down on your knees if you want)

"This magnificent Father who parcels out all heaven and earth."

(deep breath; focus on who God is)

"I ask Him to strengthen me by His Spirit."

(breathe)

"Not a brute strength but a glorious inner strength."

(deep breath)

"That Christ will live in me as I open the door and invite Him in."

(breathe deep and imagine opening the door to your heart and soul and receiving Him into yourself)

"I ask and choose now to receive the extravagant dimensions of Christ's love."

(say "thank you" as you take another deep breath)

"I reach out and experience the breadth of this love."

(breathe)

"I reach out and experience the length of this love."

(breathe)

"I reach out and experience the depth of this love."

(breathe)

"I reach out and experience the height of this love."

(breathe)

"I choose to live a life full in the fullness of God."

(deep breath)

This is my prayer for you today. Don't hurry through this. Repeat these declarations as you feel led. This is how we ought to pray a blessing for every person on earth. It is only through intimacy with Christ that we can be transformed to love supernaturally as we receive the supernatural.

CHAPTER 14

Faith

The town I live in is about twenty minutes from two Costco Wholesale stores—one in Westlake Village and the other in Oxnard. The store I patronize on any given day depends on what other errands or plans I have that day. Westlake Village is an affluent community, while Oxnard is not. The Oxnard store is in a rougher area, but that's not usually a problem for me.

This day, I finished my shopping and checked out, then realized I was starving. I'm one of those people whose blood sugar can drop suddenly, and I _need_ to eat. Costco has a pretty good chicken Caesar salad, so I decided to get some food. The prepared food setup is outside at the Oxnard store, so that's where I was. As I walked toward the crowded food lines, I noticed a young man, last in line, facing backward toward me as I approached. He had distinct tattoos on his neck and above his eyebrows. Tattoos on the face always scream "gang member" to me. I don't even know if I'm right about that, but that's what went through my head.

As I got closer to him, I could see he was physically hurt. He had scrapes and bruises on his face and neck. His eyes were swollen. It looked like he'd been in a serious fight. And there came the Holy Spirit shove—I mean nudge. Looking at the situation naturally, I should have kept my distance, chosen a different line, and stayed on guard. But Holy Spirit told me to pray for him and not just to say a quiet prayer. Jesus wanted me to pray over him. He needed prayer, but I did not want to.

Since he was facing me, I looked him straight in the eyes, mustered my kindest and most confident smile, said hello, and asked him how he was doing. In a strange, raspy voice, as if his vocal cords were damaged, he said he was good. Then he moved aside and offered for me to go ahead of him. This surprised me. Nobody lets someone go ahead of them in a food line. I took him up on his offer, momentarily thinking maybe I had misjudged him. I still felt the call to pray for him, but I was feeling something sinister too. Fear was creeping in a bit more.

I continued to wrestle with the Lord as I stood in front of him in line. I could feel his eyes on me and decided not to pray over him. I figured it was enough to just hold a loving place in my heart and pray quietly for him. I say "enough" because this was a challenge for me. I really didn't want to do this. But one thing I've learned is that whatever Holy Spirit tells me to do for some- one else is less about my relationship with the person and more about my rela- tionship with Jesus. I was fully aware that I was in a wrestling match with God. God told me to turn and pray over this man, and my flesh said, "I don't want to. He's scary. What if I just hold love for him and pray quietly for him? I mean, c'mon, God, you obviously know that he's sketchy?" But God quietly repeated His request. I ignored Him.

And I was glad I did because when I went to the drink-dispensing area to fill my soda cup, the man was watching me. While I sat and ate my salad, he hung around, awkwardly averting his eyes every time I glanced his way. And I began to regret wearing my large diamond ring and carrying my fine Ital- ian leather purse. My friend's mother-in-law had been mugged by a seemingly nice man who offered to put her groceries into her car, then grabbed her purse and ran. My friend emphasized how the criminal had probably scoped her out by her jewels, purse, and car. I felt stupid, but I thought, "Duh, God! This guy is dangerous!"

I finished my salad and tried to fool myself into thinking I wasn't afraid to walk away from the crowd and to my car. The man was still hanging around the eating area but not eating. I started toward my car with my basket full of giant packages of toilet paper and power greens for my morning shakes and a few impulse purchases.

Instinctively, I glanced back, and there he was, hot on my heels, obviously following me now. There was no denying it. I wasn't safe. Without a thought, I did the smartest thing I could've done. (By the way, I am not smart in a crisis or scary situation. I'm the person in the horror movie you're yelling at to just run away!) But what happened next really wasn't me. I acted without a single thought as if Holy Spirit had intervened on my behalf.

I turned around and faced him straight on, smiled big, and said, "There you are! I was hoping to talk to you." See God shoving me now? "I wanted to ask how you are because you look like someone has hurt you."

"I'm fine," he said guardedly, his head and shoulders retreating from me ever so slightly. "How are you?"

"I'm good."

"Where you from? Are you from Oxnard?"

Okay, that's a weird question. "No, I'm from Newbury Park."

"Is it nice there?"

"Yes, it's very nice."

"Good. Good." He said awkwardly, stalling for an idea.

I knew somehow that he wanted to walk me to my car, and he said so.

"Where are you parked? Let's walk."

"No, we can stay here and talk. Are you sure you're okay? Because you look like you've been in a fight. Can I pray for you?" *Okay, God, you win, as usual.*

"Sure, sure. You can pray for me."

"Okay, because Holy Spirit told me to pray for you."

I hadn't even gotten the sentence completely out of my mouth, and the guy turned and practically ran away from me as if the mention of Holy Spirit repulsed him or scared him. I stood there a bit dumbfounded as I watched him scuttle away.

A momentary wondering of what had just happened instantaneously produced a clear knowing as Holy Spirit answered my internal question swiftly. It came in the typical spirit talk that I usually receive . . . part words, part pictures, part knowledge. Mind you, I cannot prove any of this, but I *know* it was real.

At that moment, I *knew* that the demonic spirit on him knew he was no match for Holy Spirit, so it fled. I *knew* that the young man was Catholic by birth and culture and did not want to hurt a woman who heard from the Holy Ghost on his account. I *knew* his grandmother prays for him and that her prayers to stop him from doing things he regrets were being answered. I just *knew* all of that. I don't know how, but I did. Yay, God!

I chuckled to myself and shook my head in amazement. I said aloud: "All praises to You, Holy Spirit! Gang members can't touch me. Who can be against me? Whom shall I fear? Thank You for protecting me again." (See Romans 8:31 and Psalm 27:1.)

This story illustrates how fear can keep us from heeding God's voice. I was afraid of this guy, and reason and logic would say that made perfect sense. My son, Nick, wasn't excited upon hearing this story. He told me not to be stupid. I tried to reassure him by telling him that I intended to listen to Holy Spirit, and that if anything bad happened to me (like I ended up murdered or something drastic like that), he could know that I was good in heaven with Jesus and had no regrets. My assurances were apparently ineffective because his response was typical for a young man in his twenties. He said, "That's fine for you, Mom. But I'm going to have to hunt the guy down and kill him." *Greaaat.*

This story also shows how even after gaining so much freedom from fear, as I had already done, Jesus wanted to eliminate fear entirely from me. I had been feeling free of daily anxieties and even many of my previous fears regarding my family of origin. But Holy Spirit wanted me completely free—even of scary criminal types. We only get free and freer by walking out freedom. If I hadn't faced the fear that day, I would not have left the situation as free. I would've done the logical thing, which would've kept me from breaking through to the next level of freedom.

I also love the way this testimony illustrates God's show-off moves. He knits together our lives in complex ways to accomplish His good will for our lives: mine, the young man's, and his grandmother's (Romans 8:28). What the enemy meant for bad, God used for good (Genesis 50:20). And even though I was reluctant, ultimately, I obeyed Him, which was essential to the super cool result.

Fear Hinders Love

As Christians, we often tell ourselves that worry and fear are normal "under the circumstances." This is wrong. I'm not saying it's wrong ever to feel worry, fear, or pain. Experiencing those emotions is part of being human in this broken world. But being stuck in such feelings and cultivating a lifestyle around them is not freedom in Christ. It is bondage, no matter what you believe about Jesus. We are not to dwell in fear and worry. We are to walk out a lifestyle of faith because fear enslaves humans.

As a therapist, I saw firsthand that most of what caused dysfunction in my clients' lives was fear. I specialized in treating eating disorders, and I witnessed my clients' lives being completely fear-driven—fear of getting fat, fear of food, fear of fat in food, fear of the mirror, fear of the scale, fear of others' opinions, fear of being seen, fear of failure, fear of rejection, fear of humiliation—the list goes on and on.

And their parents and loved ones also came with their own fears that caused them to lash out or try to control or disconnect and reject. Not until they stopped operating in fear could the dance of their interactions change from being a sick downward spiral that left each one drowning in more fear and despair.

I had a wise colleague who was somewhat of a mentor. We worked together at a residential treatment center for eating disorders. She used a phrase often that stuck with me. She said that our clients, and people in general, do what they do to "bind anxiety." That's clinical terminology, and it helped me throughout my career to look at my clients' behaviors from that perspective.

But it's also an interesting, even paradoxical play on words. I would say we are bound by anxiety. My clients and most people set out to keep their anxieties bound up when we really need to get free from the anxiety binding us.

So, what does fear look like in your life if you don't have a clinical diagnosis (or even if you do)? It could be more like chronic worry that steals the present moment for years at a time. It could even be so subtle that you don't know it's there. Are you afraid something bad will happen if you or your children or loved ones don't dot every *i* and cross every *t*?

Fear is the only thing that gets smaller
the closer you get to it.

I was afraid my children would be influenced by this very fallen world, which would lead them to poor decisions and sad, painful lives. I was afraid I'd fail as a mother by being a bad example. I was afraid I would parent from fear. I knew I struggled with fear and was afraid I could not get free from it and that it would hurt my children. Fear is a pervasive foe. I believe it affects us all. We cannot talk about faith or freedom without zeroing in on freedom from fear.

Just as fear grows and destroys more and more, freedom from fear also grows. I am delivered from fear more each time I face it with faith in the One more powerful than fear. There's a great quote I used to share with my clients: "Fear is the only thing that gets smaller the closer you get to it." I used to encourage my clients to face their fears with this quote. But in my own life, I didn't want to be close to people like my family—alcoholics, drug addicts, people missing teeth, people on the street, poor, homeless, and clinically psychotic (meaning they are out of touch with reality, plagued by delusional, auditory, and visual hallucinations).

As God began to release me from fear, I felt a pull toward those exact people. In my flesh, I don't like those people. They scare me. They're unpredictable and untrustworthy. They don't smell good. They're dirty. They lie and manipulate. I have no idea what to do with these people except stay as far away as possible from them. But Holy Spirit kept nudging me toward them even when I wasn't totally full of His Love like I was with the guy in Hollywood. Despite my fear of these people, I began to press into Holy Spirit, asking exactly what He wanted me to do.

I sensed that I was to find out their names *(oh great, I have to talk to them)* and call them by name. The idea felt like the Father wanted them to know that He knew their names. He wanted them to know that their identity mattered to Him, that they were not forgotten. I also sensed Him asking me to give them a token of His Love, which to me was sustenance. So, I made muffins and gave them little packages of food and water.

I was afraid to walk up to people passed out on the sidewalk or who were holding up signs on street corners begging for money. But I knew the Lord was working in me, and I wanted to grow in my relationship with Him. I wanted His transformation. I also knew this assignment was tied to my family of origin. It was an aspect of breaking free from the generational pain of my family line. In His powerfully paradoxical way, the Father was making me more His daughter—giving me a new bloodline by calling me to love the very thing from which I was striving to break free.

The first time I ventured out in obedience to this call, I took my youngest son with me. "Joey," I asked, "would you come with me to talk to homeless people? You can just sit in the car and call for help if someone attacks me."

"Why are you wanting to talk to homeless people?"

"Well, I don't really want to, but Holy Spirit told me to go find out their names and give them His Love."

"Okay, Mom," he said with a chuckle and a tone that communicated, *Sounds like one of your wild words from God.* "Yeah, I'll go with you."

My tummy was full of butterflies as I approached a man lying on the sidewalk, who was apparently asleep. Weirdly, I noticed a fear of rejection as I approached him. When he opened his eyes, they were blue and beautiful. I asked him his name, which was John. He graciously accepted the introduction and food. I still think about him and pray for him. His eyes pierced me. I felt like the Lord was saying, "See how beautiful these people are? They are in chains, and I love them. Love them! Do not despise or fear them." I was changed.

Faith Is Essential

These are stories of faith despite fear. Faith is essential to the pursuit and mystery of freedom from generational pain. The Bible says, "Now faith is being sure of what we hope for and certain of what we do not see" (Hebrews 11:1). I love this simple definition of faith. The book of Hebrews, chapter eleven, is dedicated to the workings of faith in the lives of so many historical figures who broke free from the painful generational patterns of their generation and those of their ancestors.

Think of Abraham, who left his native land and traveled hundreds of miles to establish a new people entirely by faith. There was no precedent for him to consider. Yet, the Jewish people descended from him and his "barren" old wife (Genesis 12–21). Or Rahab, a prostitute in Jericho, who, by faith, hid the Israelite spies and helped them to return to their camp safely. Because of her actions, she and her family were spared when Jericho was conquered (Joshua 2:1–24).

These are just two of the people mentioned who changed the trajectory of their familial line profoundly. But they had to take steps of faith, often monumental steps, to manifest the generational freedom.

If you want to be challenged, read the examples of faith in Hebrews 11:1–40. Is there any circumstance in your life that requires more faith than theirs? I'm guessing not. I know I could not boast about any circumstance in my life. Allow the stories of these great heroes of the faith to sink in and inspire your faith.

Yes, faith is essential. It's necessary when expecting freedom and transformation, and interactive prayer. You have to have it to navigate daily challenges and huge life disappointments. So how does one attain faith? Three of the most important lessons I've learned about faith are that acting in faith is how we grow in faith, faith is a gift from God, and we can ask for more faith when we need it. These three principles changed my entire life, my walk with Jesus, and every relationship I have. For real!

Acting in Faith

When Amanda was dating Steven, I was plagued with fear, and faith was fleeting. I could hardly sleep. I don't think I got a decent night's sleep for at least two years. I had to fall asleep praying. Otherwise, my mind would ruminate on every hurt and loss I had endured so far and worry about what was to come. It was pretty standard for me to wake up every hour. Each time, immediate thoughts of the worst-case scenario for Amanda would play out in my mind like a sick horror film called *A Mother's Worst Nightmare*. I would start down that road of all the awful things that had already happened or could happen. Unless I prayed, I remained stuck there, like in purgatory.

Each time, I prayed away the spirit of fear that was rooted in me and asked Holy Spirit to fill me instead with love, faith, and hope. I would have a moment's peace, then my mind would wander back to fear. Again, I would have to pray myself back to sleep. Until I fell asleep, I was utterly afraid, lonely, and soul sick. Sometimes, I would just give up and get out of bed. In those moments, I figured one of two things was happening. Either Holy Spirit was waking me up to pray because prayer was needed to combat whatever schemes the devil was planning, or I just needed to be alert and conscious to take these hellish thoughts captive and resist the devil so that he would flee from me.

Faith requires trusting that God's ways are best even when they don't make sense to us. That is submitting to God's authority.

The best part is that once the devil did flee, it was just me and Jesus and sweet, intimate fellowship. And this was an utterly peaceful feeling of complete well-being. But I had to pursue that. I had to turn away from the devil's story and destiny and turn toward the destiny Christ has planned for my family and me. This required work, discipline, and tenacity because almost everything I saw in the natural world said the devil's plans were happening.

Somewhere during those sleepless nights, I listened to someone teaching about the spirit of fear. The person said that "Satan's worst fear is when we submit ourselves fully to God's authority." That submission is an act of faith. We try to do things in our own strength because we don't trust anyone else to come through for us. We do things our way because we think our ways are better. Faith requires trusting that God's ways are best even when they don't make sense to us. That is submitting to God's authority.

I was so sick and tired of being tossed, torn, and tortured by fear that I decided to fully submit to God's authority. "Take that, devil! You lose! Who's afraid now?! Huh? Huh!" That decision was to be tested for sure. The enemy attempted to mock me and tell me I was not capable of an all-out surrender to God's authority. And it was through this process that I learned about death—death to self.

One of the ways I practice self-death and submitting to God's authority is by praising God, always reaching toward God, and seeking intimacy with Him. I do not entertain or give life to the gods of emotions and fear that my natural mind and body experience, no matter what I see in the natural. Instead, I pray for more faith and give those fears and the pain of the situation to Jesus, sometimes multiple times per hour.

Essentially, acting in faith means not giving power or headspace to these emotions and thoughts. It means not even giving voice to them except to the Lord or someone like Barbara, who will point us upward with them. So, until Holy Spirit showed me who He was in this messiness of life and gave me a new perspective in the form of peace, joy, and love toward all parties, I stayed low. "Do not act from any other place besides faith," Barbara would say.

Kneeling on the sidelines of my daughter's early adult life, Barbara often told me to keep my eyes on Jesus, to stop focusing on the natural, and to pray for victory in the spirit realm. And I tried. I spoke words and prayers of faith by faith, but the gift of faith was not yet deposited deep within me. Therefore, I continued to suffer. I had to act in faith. I took every fearful thought captive and conformed it to the will of God (2 Corinthians 10:5). Whenever I became aware that I was ruminating over some decision my daughter had made and the potential outcomes of that decision, I took those thoughts captive in prayer and attempted to kick them out of my head.

It looked something like this: "Jesus, I repent for partnering with a spirit of fear. I choose to partner with faith right now. Therefore, I trust You with my daughter. I give my daughter to You. I release my daughter fully into your care, knowing You love her more than I love her, and You are fighting for her. I choose faith over fear, and I command fear to leave and loose me now."

There were many days when I prayed that prayer several times every hour, all day long. I simply could not sustain a faith-filled perspective. The earth was so heavy that I could not find heaven. Everything I saw in the natural world— the things happening all around me—tempted me, and I often succumbed to doubt and unbelief.

So, I continued to pray: "I repent for partnering with a spirit of doubt and unbelief. I choose to walk faithfully with You, Jesus. I choose to trust You with my daughter's life. I choose to believe and not doubt that You are working in this situation no matter how hopeless it looks in the natural. I believe You are moving in the spirit realm to redeem this situation. You are good."

Again, I was acting in faith, which was an amazing discipline and kept me at the feet of Jesus all day long. One day, while I was listing to Barb all the distressing things my daughter had been doing, she gave me a crazy assignment. Mind you, I did not tell many people what was going on with Amanda, but Barb was my one safe place to share. We talked often, so she got the play-by-play as I knew it and all my accompanying worries. I think that sometimes morphed into an unconscious tug for validation from her for my fear and worry. She did not bite. Instead, she said,

"Rena, radical gratitude! Every time you find out something that worries you, or you begin to go into fear about things you already know, I want you to thank God for that very thing."

"What? Like, thank God that Amanda is dating an ex-gang member?"

"Yep! Whatever the thought or new piece of information, thank God. Radical gratitude."

She was asking me to walk out that Scripture that says: "Rejoice always, pray continually, give thanks in all circumstances; for this is God's will for you in Christ Jesus" (1 Thessalonians 5:16–18). *Do what the Bible says.* That's a tough one. But as usual, for that time period, I was so desperate. I had nothing of my own to help me. So I did it by faith. And it was weird.

"Thank you, God, that my relationship with Amanda is broken."

"Thank you, God, that . . ."

It was a long chain of disappointment and fear and failure. I kept thanking God for every single one. Weird. But even weirder, it relaxed me. I think it was a surrender. Yes, it was yet another death to my will and my striving. I accepted what was and gave radical gratitude. This was powerful medicine for my anxious heart and a master's level faith walk-out. I was acting in faith on a whole new level.

Faith Is a Gift

Ephesians 2:8 (NKJV) says, "For by grace you have been saved through faith, and that not of yourselves; it is the gift of God, not of works that anyone should boast."

I used to read that Scripture and focus on the word grace. Of course, salvation through Christ takes faith, but grace is such a beautiful aspect of Christianity. I liked to hang out there. Then I heard a teacher explain how that passage also says that faith is a gift of God. I always thought faith was a decision or a choice. The idea of faith being a gift caused me to pause and consider whether or not I had the gift of faith. I believed in Jesus. But did I have faith? No, I did not.

Faith is a supernatural thing. Jesus said that if we had faith as small as a mustard seed, we could move a mountain (Matthew 17:20–21). Mark 5:25–34 tells about a woman who was healed by merely touching Jesus's garment because of the faith she had that she would be healed. Jesus felt the power go out of Him and told the woman, "Daughter, your faith has made you well; go and be healed of your affliction" (v. 34 NKJV). This woman had been hemorrhaging for twelve years and had endured much at the hands of her physicians to no avail. But she had faith and received a miracle.

I did not have that kind of faith, and I knew I needed it.

Asking for and Receiving Faith

About this time, I happened to be working through a teaching on faith. The workbook was filled with Scripture after Scripture on faith. They were organized by topics. (I have included part of the list at the end of the chapter for your reference.) The teacher said we could ask for faith because faith was a gift from God that He would bestow upon us if we asked. I needed that gift desperately, so I prayed and asked for the gift of faith . . . then went about my day still anxious with the need to pray all day as usual.

The next day, I asked for faith again and asked what was blocking the gift. I felt Holy Spirit encourage me to go back to the teaching and read every Scripture, pray every Scripture, and meditate on every Scripture, gleaning what He would have to teach me from them. Desperate as usual, I dug into that assignment. It definitely could not hurt.

It took me two weeks of one-hour sessions in the wee hours of the morning in my little library, but I read every one of those Scriptures and wrote them out, or at least paraphrased them so that I was sure to get the message. It was a sweet two weeks of soaking in the teachings of faith. I prayed the Scriptures as best I could.

I would read: "[Now] faith is being sure of what you hope for and certain of what you do not see" (Hebrews 11:1). Then I would pray, "Dear Jesus, I am sure of what I hope for, and I am certain of what I do not see. I am sure You are preparing a beautiful future for my daughter. I am certain she is learning and growing and that her choices are shaping her for Your kingdom come."

I wrote something like that for virtually every passage. When I couldn't see how to pray the Scripture, I just repeated it, took deep breaths, and repeated it again. I meditated on the words. Meditation often brought Holy Spirit prayers flowing from my lips. Abiding with what the word of God says about faith produced a miracle of faith in me.

The gift did not come right away. I had to persevere and relentlessly pursue God for it. Each morning after meditating on and praying these Scriptures, I would cry out to God for the gift of faith. I used language like beg, cry out, desperately plead, and beseech. Through tears of desperation, I literally begged God every morning and then lived each day in fear without faith. I reminded Him of the parable Jesus told of the widow who kept pestering the ungodly judge for justice. Every day, she begged him for protection. Finally, he gave it to her because he did not want to be bothered with her anymore (Luke 18:1–6).

Jesus concluded this parable by saying:

"Will not God bring about justice for his chosen ones, who cry out to Him day and night? Will he keep putting them off? I tell you, he will see that they get justice, and quickly. However, when the Son of Man comes, will He find faith on the earth?" (Luke 18:7–8)

I followed the example of the widow, begging day and night for faith. And God was faithful. When it came, I knew I had the gift of faith.

Fear left. Joy came in.

Faith is so fun because whatever I experienced in the natural world—literally, whatever happened, whatever choices my daughter made—I truly trusted God to make it right in the end. It's kind of like when you know the story has a happy ending and the protagonist survives the plane crash; you're not sad and upset while you're watching the plane go down.

It was awesome, I'm telling you. He is so good. He is faithful. Just go get Him. Seek Him. Because as I read and wrote down His words, Holy Spirit would reveal the specific message He wanted to tell me personally through His Word. I wrote those down, too, and still refer to them when I am in a rough patch. God's Word is living and powerful to change us. Do not underestimate this. I encourage you to take time today with these Scriptures and ask Holy Spirit to reveal His personal message to you through His Word.

Spending time with Holy Spirit—reading, writing, and meditating on Scriptures of faith and persistently praying for faith—was the catalyst for me to receive the gift of faith.

Spurred on by Faith

Anxiety, fear, and worry are sinister weapons that keep so many in chains. If we could only get *free* from all anxiety, we would be unrecognizable as a species. What if we didn't fear others' opinions? What if we were so filled with the Love of Christ that even a menacing criminal could not stir up fear within us?

Remember the story about the man in Hollywood who verbally assaulted me and showed physical aggression toward me? I was completely free from fear that day. Truly, supernaturally free. And look at the result. The situation could've devolved into one where my son or my husband might have physically hurt the man in my defense. It could've been just a spectacle on the street of us hurrying away while he yelled obscenities at us, which would've impacted everyone on that crowded boulevard. That would've spread ugliness, despair, judgment, fear, and a whole host of negative energy, depending on who was listening.

Instead, because I was filled with Jesus and, therefore, totally free from fear, love and hope were beautifully communicated and flourished out of that dark beginning. It was spurred by my faith in the mighty God of heaven and earth. My faith soared that night on the way home. I could hardly stay on earth. I felt like I just might fly, or the car could miraculously fly us home.

I had known with my head that nothing was impossible with God (Luke 1:37), but now I knew it with everything I was.

That is faith manifested. C'mon—that's crazy! And awesome! Only God does that!

Reflections on Loving

I encourage you to reflect on where you lack faith in your life. What do you worry about? What are you afraid of? What situations are you trying to control? Look for doubts and unbelief or even anger and pain. These can all be clues. Ask Holy Spirit to reveal the areas in your life where you lack faith. Pray this prayer: "Holy Spirit, show me the areas in my life where I lack faith. Where do I need to cultivate more faith in my life?"

These are some of the Scriptures I spent two weeks reading, writing, praying, and meditating on. Write down your thoughts and what you sense or feel. Consider them an invitation to begin acting on, asking for, and receiving the supernatural gift of faith.[19]

ABOUT FAITH:
ROMANS 10:8–11 ∾ HEBREWS 10:22–23

FAITH DOES:
JAMES 2:14–26

FAITH PERSEVERES:
ISAIAH 62:6,7 ∾ HEBREWS 11 ∾ LUKE 18:1–8
1 PETER 1:7 ∾ ACTS 14:22

FAITH RESTS:
PSALM 46:10 ∾ HEBREWS 4:1–12

EVIDENCE OF FAITH:
LUKE 7:50 ∾ ACTS 14:8–10

FAITH HEALS:
MARK 10:52 ∾ MATTHEW 9:22 ∾ LUKE 5:20

LITTLE OR NO FAITH:
MATTHEW 6:30 ∾ LUKE 8:2

GREAT FAITH:
MATTHEW 8:5–10 ∾ MATTHEW 15:21–28

DON'T DOUBT:
MATTHEW 21:21 ∾ JAMES 1:6

INCREASE FAITH:
2 THESSALONIANS 1:3 ∾ 2 CORINTHIANS 10:15 ∾ LUKE 17:5

FULL OF FAITH:
ACTS 6:5 ∾ HEBREWS 10:22

UNFAILING FAITH:
REVELATION 2:13

UNITY OF FAITH:
EPHESIANS 4:13

CHAPTER 15

Forgiveness

*I*t was a victorious day at Amanda's wedding. Truly, I was glowing. She was glowing, too, of course, but for different reasons. I was glowing because I was full of the presence of the Lord. He had filled me with His peace, joy, and love so much that it poured out of me, and I was shining with His love. It was, indeed, supernatural. The day was a culmination of two-plus years of disappointment, pain, and mockery, yet I was there in body with an open heart to love and cherish each person there. I relished in the power of Holy Spirit to overcome and heal brokenness.

We stayed in a motel that night located about halfway from home. I went to sleep easily enough, but in the wee hours of the morning, I jolted up in bed with a loud groan as if a knife had just been plunged into my heart. All at once, I saw the present and future of Franklin, my step-grandson, and my future grandchildren. It was a horrific vision filled with repetitive cursing words. It's hard to explain because a vision is somewhat like a dream, yet I was awake.

The pictures and words were clear as day. You know how dreams can seem nonsensical when you're trying to relay them to someone else while making perfect sense before you try to describe them? This vision was like that.

What I saw was terrible, and I felt hopeless. I was helpless to stop what my future grandchildren would suffer. The vision contained everything I thought I had broken free from. The devil told me I was an anomaly and his plans would reign in my generational line. I was repeatedly shown that any attempt I made to save or help was going to blow up in my face, just as my numerous attempts to stop Amanda from marrying Steven had done. This vision occurred on Easter Sunday, 2016.

I now know that it was a lie from hell. This was the devil's plan for my posterity. I don't like to give space and energy to hell, but I need to explain its relentless nature. I want to be transparent in how I share the process of breaking generational bondage. Familiar spirits don't let go easily, and sometimes we are taken in by them again and again.

But that doesn't mean the situation is hopeless. It doesn't mean you've lost. Keep pressing into God for more freedom, and let His family DNA course through your spiritual veins and on into the generations to follow. It is a battle, and God's angels are fighting for you. The victory is the Lord's, and you are His daughter or son, so you must keep persevering.

With that truth in mind, let me share how I moved through this situation. It wasn't pretty. In short, I was transported into a region of deep captivity on a spiritual level. That may sound super weird, but that's what it felt like. In an instant, I went from living in a victorious, loving place of wholeness and freedom to being a chained-up, embittered, hopeless wretch.

We drove to a friend's church before going to my sister-in-law's house for Easter dinner. I asked my husband to please take me home instead. The life had drained out of me, and I could not bear church or a family gathering. He wouldn't do it. He said he thought I needed to go to church and be with family. Isolating was not good for me. I disagreed, so I refused to go in when he and my son went into the church. Instead, I surrendered to my inner despair. Or I suffered in it. It didn't feel like I had a choice. The lies were thick, and I could not see through them.

I was in the garden of Gethsemane, sweating blood. Not to denigrate what Jesus went through there, since He was taking on the debt of the entire creation and every person ever. Clearly, that was astronomically more challenging than anything I was suffering. But He is God. I am just me . . . some woman in California. Seeing this awful fate of my family and having zero power to change it grieved me to the core. I did not want that cup. I could not bear that cup. I was alone and saw myself in chains in a pit. Here is a journal excerpt that gives a glimpse of my torture:

> God, I cannot feel You at all. I'm locked in. I'm so angry at You for leaving me in this impossible situation. I just don't trust You anymore. I'm so sad and feel pointless, ugly, lost, and terrible.
>
> Everywhere I turn, I feel unworthy. Yes, I feel forsaken, unloved, even hated. I remember Your peace, but I can't have it now.
>
> I'm supposed to ask what You say to all of this. I just feel pressure on my chest in a bad way. No answer. I hate You, God. I hate You, God. You're so mean!

Then the faintest whisper came to me. Even in that dark place, Holy Spirit spoke to me: "You won't listen to Me if I answer. You don't believe."

That was true. That was the only true thing at that moment. As I write this, it still amazes me how fragile my spiritual state was. I crashed so hard, so fast. Remember, this was one day after that incredible spiritual high of Amanda's wedding day.

The month that followed was ugly. I became angry and hateful toward Steven. I did not say anything to him, but my thoughts were hideous and intrusive. As I feared the vision was prophecy, and as I played out this future over and over, I simply wanted Steven dead. It was so crazy. I really am a loving person . . . usually. I shared these rantings with my mentor. She patiently listened, then spoke truth to me. But I was unmoved.

Freedom through Forgiveness

I promise I will finish this story and tell you how forgiveness was the key to escaping the prison of hate and hopelessness. But first, I need to talk to you in some depth about forgiveness.

In his letter to the Ephesian church, the apostle Paul wrote, "Get rid of all bitterness, rage and anger, brawling and slander, along with every form of malice" (Ephesians 4:31). This exhortation does not exactly include the word forgive, but it strongly implies it. Breaking free from bitterness, rage, etc., requires forgiveness.

My unforgiveness toward my family of origin clouded my entire life and, therefore my ability to make life decisions. On a deeper level it produced rottenness and bitter fruit.

Freedom seems to hinge on forgiveness. Maybe it's just me. Perhaps I'm just a terrible grudge-holder, constantly keeping records of wrongs and obsessing about every wrong that has been transgressed against me. Yes. Those things have been true of me, and I need to discipline myself to maintain a lifestyle of forgiveness to remain free. But freedom and forgiveness are not typically linked in our society. We admire forgiveness. We consider it a virtue, mainly because we know it's difficult. We often say certain atrocities are "unforgivable." So, yes, we admire and esteem forgiveness. But when we think of freedom, forgiveness is not typically in the picture. Freedom is not a virtue. It's more of a right and a privilege, even an aspiration.

We usually go after freedom by getting out of some bad situation or moving to a freer society. We call freedom "the right to choose" or "the right to bear arms." We fight wars—literally, we bury thousands of our sons and daughters in cold graves—to free others from evil dictators and ensure they don't get too close to our shores. That is not the kind of freedom I link to forgiveness. I'm talking about deep-in-your-soul freedom. I'm talking about total spiritual freedom. Freedom that does not depend on circumstances. I wanted freedom from my family of origin. I did get away from those problems geographically and lived my life absent of my family-of-origin issues. I protected my children from just about every whisper of those problems. But I was not free.

I've already challenged you to do what the Bible says. So what does the Bible say about forgiveness?

Truths about Forgiveness

God Forgives

You, Lord, are forgiving and good, abounding in love to all who call to you.
(Psalm 86:5)

∽

For I will forgive their wickedness and will remember their sins no more.
(Hebrews 8:12)

These verses clearly state, repeatedly, what God offers us. He remembers our offenses no more. They no longer exist. Wow! God models for us how to forgive others and even ourselves, which I will delve into in the next chapter. These Scriptures reveal how completely He forgives us.

God's Forgiveness Saves Us

He has delivered us from the power of darkness and conveyed
us into the kingdom of the Son of His love, in whom we have
redemption through His blood, the forgiveness of sins.
(Colossians 1:13–14 nkjv)

A core tenet of Christianity is that we need God's forgiveness to be reconciled to Him. This verse states this clearly.

Love and Forgiveness Are Connected

Love prospers when a fault is forgiven, but
dwelling on it separates close friends.
(Proverbs 17:9 nlt)

This is so good. So true. When we forgive, Love prospers. The opposite is also true, sadly. When we do not forgive, Love shrinks, and judgment and pride grow. Do you want to be a judgmental, prideful person? If not, you must completely forgive every person of every offense from the heart. This is no small or easy task, but it's true.

FORGIVENESS MAY BE TRANSACTIONAL

Do not judge, and you will not be judged. Do not condemn, and
you will not be condemned. Forgive, and you will be forgiven.
(Luke 6:37)

Several Scriptures link our forgiveness towards others as a precursor to God's forgiveness toward us. This is challenging because I thought that God forgives no matter what. The Bible speaks so clearly about God's mercy and grace towards us, culminating in complete forgiveness of every sin ever committed. Yet, this Scripture, and others like it (Matthew 6:1–14), seem to say that forgiveness is conditional. This is how Holy Spirit has taught me regarding this idea.

This Scripture emphasizes the symbiotic relationship between forgiving others and receiving Jesus's forgiveness. Secondly, they point out the power of forgiveness to bring favor in your life. It's like those Scriptures that say to be above reproach so that even your enemy cannot speak ill against you (1 Peter 2:12; Titus 2:8). If I am careful in my mind, heart, and words—because, remember, "out of the abundance of the heart the mouth speaks" (Matthew 12:34 ESV)—then I am less likely to have people judge, condemn, or harbor bitterness towards me. It's not a guarantee, but if I judge others and condemn others, you'd better believe they will pounce on the opportunity to judge me should something negative come to light in my life.

Boy, did I learn this the hard way. I spent so many years raising my family in a particular way that I truly believed was superior to the culture. I homeschooled and unabashedly infused my children's education with the Bible and a biblical worldview based on Western civilization. I was careful about what my children consumed in media and pop culture. We did not have a television in our home for ten years. If I hadn't first screened a movie or show, my children weren't allowed to watch it. But there were those more liberal parents who allowed their children to watch various things that I considered crude and lacked any substantive value. Why allow that garbage into my children's minds? So, I didn't—and I couldn't understand the passive manner of so many parents who did not hold the same standards.

I didn't consciously set out to judge people. I was just trying to do the right thing in my life. But judge, I did. I told myself I was a more conscientious parent. I was willing to fight for my children's hearts more than so and so was. I was investing in what was really important.

Those thoughts weren't so bad, except they were replete with pride. I know this because right after those thoughts, others came, like, "How could so-and-so allow her kids to do that? Or see that? Or participate in that?" *Judgment!* I was judging. Honestly, I was in denial of my own sin here. I earnestly rationalized (if you can do that) that I was standing up for God's righteous best. Sometimes it blows my mind how easily I can be deceived.

So, when my daughter publicly began to go off the path we had carefully set before her, people judged her and us. Not everyone. But many did. And it hurt. But as the Lord began to sanctify me, He showed me how I had brought that judgment upon myself. I'm tempted, even now, to talk about how wrong those who judged me were, but that's a judgment against them.

Judgment, bitterness, and unforgiveness are subtle, relentless foes. They creep in, often undetected, and take up residence in your heart and mind until they have clear control of your word and deed. And they had taken up residency in me.

So the Lord demanded that I repent for all judgment and that I forgive them for judging me. It was so hard. That's an understatement. It was one of those death-to-self moments, which I'll explain more about later. There I was in agony and prayer for my most prized gift, my daughter. People who knew us well, people who had been close to us, were judging her and our family. They were making up worse things in their minds about us than what was true—but God was telling me to repent for every time I had judged. He showed me times I had judged that I had forgotten. He pointed with laser sharpness at how judgment had weaseled its way into my soul until I could no longer deny it. I could only choose to stay in judgment or repent. So repent, I did.

I had brought this judgment upon myself by judging others. I needed to repent for judgment and turn around and forgive those judging me. Really, truly forgive them. Otherwise, I would remain stuck in that vicious cycle of judgment and unforgiveness, an ugly downward spiral into a very dark abyss.

And it started with my judgment against my family of origin. I had judged them harshly, beginning with my mother when I was fourteen when she let me down in that very painful way. I wrote her angry letters full of judgment, ranting to her about what a terrible mother she was. I told her how sick and deranged and weak she was!

As a therapist, I know that my anger was justified and that a fourteen-year-old girl who had just been wounded and abandoned by her mother is completely valid in feeling righteous anger and deep hurt. That was not the sin. *The sin was the judgment, refusal to forgive, and pride that came along for the ride.* From that moment on, I began a very long pattern of judging people who resembled my family of origin in any way. I thought ill of them. I spoke ill of them, and I treated them as if they had the plague. Talk about "social distancing."

Ultimately, I was deceived into thinking that if I stayed away from people resembling my family of origin, that would somehow break the generational patterns in my precious children's lives and generational lines.

> As long as I hold onto any offense,
> my freedom is limited.

But, as usual, God turns human reasoning upside down. In His infinite, cosmic, paradoxical way, Jesus showed me that I would have to forgive, love, and embrace the very things I wanted to break free from. As I chose to forgive by an act of my will, Holy Spirit was faithful to show me my heart, and it wasn't pretty. It was full of self-righteous, prideful judgment against many of my family members. Fear ruled in my heart, and I believed the lies attached to it. The result was plain old hate.

I see now that Steven was merely a representation of my family. Therefore, he triggered all that ugliness in my heart. It was an opportunity for me to do some major inner housekeeping.

So, it was only by truly forgiving my family of origin (and anyone resembling them) and all those who had judged and hurt my daughter and me that I could truly receive Jesus's forgiveness. I know this may drive the theologians crazy. I apologize and ask you to forgive me and not judge me.

I am trying to make sense of these difficult Scriptures that say we must forgive to be forgiven. More importantly, I am merely explaining what I experienced and, therefore, fully know to be true. I know that, cosmically and existentially, Jesus does not need me to forgive my enemy before His forgiveness can be real. Yet, I also know that *to walk in the freedom reality of that forgiveness,* I have to forgive everyone—enemy, brother, sister, neighbor—everyone!

As long as I hold onto any offense, my freedom is limited. So even though Jesus forgives me, I don't *experience* that complete forgiveness as I walk around on planet earth unless I walk in forgiveness by forgiving others.

Unforgiveness Leads to Bitterness

Make every effort to live in peace with everyone and to be holy; without holiness no one will see the Lord. See to it that no one falls short of the grace of God and that no bitter root grows up to cause trouble and defile many. (Hebrews 12:14–15)

The Bible does not talk about *unforgiveness* directly very much. But it does talk quite a bit about bitterness. A quick Google search popped up thirteen verses about bitterness. The Scripture above calls bitterness a root. When we are offended and don't forgive, a root of bitterness grows in our hearts, and the ensuing fruit is rotten. It looks like resentment, gossip, curses, and judgment. It informs our reasoning about others and can become the foundation of an entire worldview. This was the case with me. My *unforgiveness* toward my family of origin clouded my entire life and, therefore, my ability to make life decisions. Sometimes it caused me to make good choices, so I thought it was good and held onto it for a long time. But on a deeper level, it produced rottenness and bitter fruit.

Forgiveness is core to the Christian faith. Forgiveness tore down the wall between humanity and the God of the universe. Forgiveness is foundational to how we need to relate to one another and even ourselves.

I was finally ready to learn how forgiveness actually happens, starting with me.

Reflections on Loving

Forgiveness is serious. It is the very thing that saves us existentially and eternally. Take a moment now to reflect.

1. When have you held onto unforgiveness, refusing to forgive someone for an extended period? Briefly summarize that story here.

_____

_____

_____

_____

_____

_____

_____

_____

2. How has unforgiveness affected:
    Your thought life?

_____

_____

_____

_____

_____

_____

_____

_____

_____

Your relationship(s)?

_____

_____

_____

_____

_____

_____

Your emotional and spiritual well-being?

_____

_____

_____

_____

_____

_____

_____

CHAPTER 16

Forgiving Yourself

Often, the first person we need to forgive is ourselves. The Love of God inside us is the very thing that empowers us to forgive others from the heart. Forgiving others is a vital precursor to walking by the Spirit, bringing Kingdom wherever you go, and breaking chains of bondage. But forgiving yourself is also crucial, and it's often harder than forgiving others. I think that is in part because we know our own hearts. We know the evil thoughts and desires that swirl within ourselves. Worse, we know God *knows* them too.

Psalm 139 tells us this—He knows our innermost thoughts. He is familiar with all of our ways, and basically, there's nowhere we can go that He cannot see us and be with us. In context, I find this chapter of the Bible to be extremely comforting, but it can also cause trepidation. Seen in the light of the fullness of the Bible, His knowing makes His forgiveness that much more complete and precious.

Believing Lies

Let's start with the lies we believe. So much of what we don't forgive ourselves for is connected to lies about who we are and what we have done. The enemy whispers (and sometimes screams) lies. We take them in and then live from those lies.

We think if we do all the right things, the results will be what we want. That doesn't sound bad at first glance, but it's a lie. And the result of this lie is self-reliance, control, and fear. Because who can do the right things all the time? And what are the right things? Who says what is right? You can say that God says what is right and consult the Bible to understand what is right, but it can't answer every question. Like, should I keep my children away from drug addicts and criminals? Or should I bring them with me to serve and love those living on the streets? Should I reject people who are "living in sin" and thereby protect my children from bad examples? Or should I embrace all people no matter what their lifestyle because Jesus spent His ministry mostly with the marginalized?

Which is it? Where is the line between protecting the innocent and embracing all people? What about the line between grace and discipline? How much should I require obedience from my children and give quick consequences for defiance? Shouldn't I teach them to respect authority? Or should I extend more grace considering their point of view in a situation, even when they are young?

As a grandma, I tend to err on the side of grace and understanding. I've been helping out in my daughter's back garden lately, and my two-year-old grandson has been "helping" me. I bought him his own little tools and gloves, and he digs and rakes and plants with me. Together, we discover worms and slugs, and he shows me when the moon is in the sky during the morning hours. We get very dirty and sometimes muddy and wet while we learn together how to fix sprinklers.

Whenever it's time for me to leave, he protests emphatically. He blocks the door and cries, saying he wants to keep working in the garden. "Avó needs to go, Hanky," I say, "but I will see you lala (later)." This does not appease him in the least. "No! I don't want you to go," he wails. This goes on even when his mama gets involved, telling him to let Avó leave. If she threatens a time-out, he just cries more earnestly.

I realize I'm telling a story of my grandson adoring me as an example of him acting defiantly. But hey, I'm a grandma. In truth, though, in those moments, he is acting bratty. But I usually sit down with him and talk with him for a bit about why he doesn't want me to go and what he wants to do. I find that if I listen to his heart and then give him something like one time playing with his cars on the carpet, which takes two minutes, then he can let me go happily. He just needs his disappointed heart to be seen and tended to a little.

My daughter thinks I spoil him and that I shouldn't respond to his bratty behavior. She says when I do just leave, he stops crying within a minute and is fine. She says he's just "working" me, and I shouldn't let him manipulate me. Maybe she is right. But that's my point. We cannot know the exact right way of parenting or grandparenting. It's a lie to believe there is one perfect way to achieve some ideal result in parenting.

I needed to repent and forgive myself for believing and acting on this lie.

As part of my journey, Barbara often led me in prayers asking Holy Spirit to reveal what lies I believed about specific situations that were upsetting me. Before this lesson and practice, I hadn't realized how much lies impacted and informed my life. I guess it shouldn't surprise me that Satan uses lies against me. He is called the "father of lies," after all.

In fact, Jesus told the religious leaders of His day that when Satan lies, "he speaks his native language, for he is a liar and the father of lies" (John 8:44). So, of course, he uses lies against us! I had never thought to pray to identify the lies I was believing or to ask Holy Spirit what the truth was. This practice helped free me from many destructive lies that kept me in emotional and spiritual chains.

One of those specific times that Barbara asked me to write down the lies I believed was right after Amanda had married Steven, and I had that terrible dream/vision. The list I made was part of setting a foundation that would allow me to forgive Steven. At the time I wrote it, I was in bondage to unforgiveness, despair, and fear. Here is what I wrote down.

Lies I believed after Amanda married Steven when I was in a pit of despair:

I'm not loved by God.

I'm forsaken by God.

I'm being punished by God for the sins of my youth

God is taking away my daughter as a punishment for having two abortions when I was seventeen—those daughters who would have blessed and honored me.

God hates me because I haven't trusted Him.

I deserve this rejection and humiliation from Amanda because I humiliated her by talking too openly about her struggles.

Amanda hates me for all the ways I hurt her growing up.

I will never have a safe, loving relationship with Amanda.

I am no longer free.

I cannot have real freedom.

It's pointless to seek God because I'll just blow it again.

There's no way I can give up the offenses Steven has trespassed against me.

God doesn't care about me or my children.

It can never be fixed.

No matter what, there's no answer.

I'm totally trapped.

There's no way out with my daughter.

I can't forgive.

I can't love.

Love is manipulated to allow evil, so I shouldn't love.

They will continue to cause pain and trauma, so I should stay away.

God will only lead me to more pain and humiliation.

I'm a failure.

I cannot please God.

I'm a fraud.

I'm a bad person.

God doesn't care about my suffering.

God cannot be trusted.

Wow. You can see the depths of the deceit I was caught in. My days were dramatically dark. Once I had the list, however, we went through it. I broke ties with each lie by praying, "I repent for believing the lie that [fill in the blank]. I renounce this lie. Holy Spirit, what is the truth?" Then I waited for Him to answer.

The truths Holy Spirit gave me during that time were sweet and acted as pure, refreshing water over my wounded soul. Lies wound. When someone lies to you, it hurts. It breaks trust. When the devil lies to us, make no mistake, it is an effort to destroy us. So, yes, it wounds. But the truth is powerful to free and heal. So, as Holy Spirit told me the truth to combat each lie, I chose to receive the truth informationally as an act of my will. Simultaneously, I received the Truth into my soul. I received Jesus more. Jesus said, "I am the way and the truth and the life" (John 14:6). Suddenly, this broken, regretful, pathetic woman (me) rested in God's Truth, confident and grateful.

As I describe here, freedom from lies and the resulting infilling of truth does not always happen immediately. I had already been on this journey with Jesus for a couple of years when I prayed through the lies listed above. I had been diligently rooting out lies and practicing forgiveness almost daily for many months. So, by the time I decided to pray through these intense lies, I already had a lot of freedom (contrary to the lie stated above). I just needed to inhabit that freedom again. At the beginning of my journey, though, I may not have experienced such an immediate release. I may have, but it's not a failure if it doesn't happen immediately. Don't believe the lie that God won't free you from lies just because it doesn't happen all at once. Keep pursuing truth, and the lies will fall away.

Forgiving Oneself (An Example)

One day, the Lord gave me a word. He said, "It's easier to repent than to forgive yourself. And it's hard to repent."

When things go wrong with our children, or when our children make scary, poor decisions, we, as parents, often feel responsible. We feel ashamed, embarrassed, and afraid. To manage the out-of-control situation, we commonly go over everything we have done so far and how most of that was terribly wrong. This process happens in a millisecond but continues incessantly, taking up every waking hour. Unless we let ourselves off the hook by forgiving ourselves, it can descend into toxic shame, fear, and a clinical major depressive episode or panic.

Since this is so important, we need to be very serious about it. Toxic shame can be so overbearing that we believe it's true, and we need someone to help us see it for what it is and guide us in self-forgiveness. I needed this for sure, and Barbara was my guide. She taught me to pray clearly to the Lord, "Holy Spirit, what do I need to forgive myself for?" Then she taught me to listen and forgive. I learned to say things like, "I choose to forgive myself for parenting from fear. I choose to forgive myself for going too fast with Amanda and not seeing her pace. I choose to forgive myself for speaking critical words over my children. I choose to forgive myself for . . ." And the list went on as Holy Spirit revealed those things I was repeatedly judging myself for.

Forgiving yourself is so fundamental to freedom because you cannot give what you do not have.

He also recalled old sin from the "Longing" section of this book. I thought I had forgiven myself for those things. I knew I was forgiven for those things. But, if the enemy can keep any smidge of self-unforgiveness hidden in some moldy crevice of our soul, he will. And he will use it to permeate and infect our ability to fully receive God's Love. In turn, our ability to freely give that same Love to others is also affected.

Finally understanding this, I went back and chose to forgive myself for all the sins of my youth and the sins of my adult life. Indeed, the list of things I needed to forgive myself for was longer than any laundry list I had against anyone else in my life.

Forgiving yourself is so fundamental to freedom because you cannot give what you do not have. Many Christians miss this and are deceived into thinking that self-forgiveness is somehow selfish. By skipping over forgiving ourselves, we keep ourselves in chains for those sins. As we continue to walk in unforgiveness, we act unforgiven. Unforgiven people are burdened and downcast and sometimes angry and apathetic. Unforgiven people have a harder time forgiving and carrying joy, peace, and love. We must forgive everyone, and that includes ourselves!

Barbara also had me list all the mistakes I thought I had made raising Amanda. So, I prayerfully asked Holy Spirit to show me the mistakes I made while raising her. My eyes opened to the excruciating reality of the ways that I had unwittingly kept my daughter tied to the bondage of my family of origin. Here's the list He gave me:

Mistakes I made raising Amanda:

I did not encourage her in her struggles.

I acted in fear by warning, controlling, and trying to fix the situation. (I thought I was advocating for her.)

My words and actions made her feel unaccepted and discouraged.

I embarrassed her by talking to others about her learning disorder (LD) to others. (I thought I was taking the shame out of it and challenging her shame.)

I felt and exhibited stress and anxiety about her LD and our home remodel.

I created a lack of security by complaining about her dad.

I did not model Jesus's love in me because of my bitterness toward others and deep hurt from my mom, dad, and husband.

I fought with Amanda instead of loving and encouraging her. (I thought I was fighting *for* her.)

I often did not see her but saw only myself instead.

I did not bless her wedding or marriage.

I went too fast all the time. She has a slower pace.

I drank too much wine to escape the stress of motherhood.

I struggled with a depressed mood and lack of joy. I was not a happy mother.

I was too rough in my interactions with her. I lacked

gentleness in words, thought, and action.

I did not have faith in Jesus. Instead, I had stress, worry, bitterness, and fear.

I did not embrace her friends due to fear.

I did not trust her wisdom and strength.

I placed the burden of my emotions on her by not containing them. (I thought I was modeling genuine personhood.)

I sinned emotionally by idolizing emotions/feelings.

I valued character over my relationship with her.

Once we had this list, we used it to pray for self-forgiveness.

"I choose to forgive myself for . . ."

One at a time, I filled in that prayer with every item listed above. We did not hurry through it. Taking deep breaths in and exhaling fully, I enacted my will to forgive myself for each mistake. In obedience to the word of God, I released myself from the bondage of these mistakes and allowed Holy Spirit to minister to me. There were tears as I released years of shame and regret.

And as my heart broke open, Holy Spirit entered with His Loving Forgiveness that separates my sin from me as far as the east is from the west. Psalm 103:1 was happening for me in real-time as I set my heart to self-forgiveness and began praising the Lord with my inmost being. Through the rest of that chapter, the words of the psalmist speak beautifully to my heart.

The LORD works righteousness and justice for all the oppressed.
(Psalm 103:6)

The LORD is compassionate and gracious, slow to anger, abounding in love.
(Psalm 103:8)

He does not treat us as our sins deserve or repay
us according to our iniquities.
(Psalm 103:10)

As far as the east is from the west, so far has he
removed our transgressions from us.
(Psalm 103:12)

———

I finally received the forgiveness that had already been there waiting for me. It was powerful and beautiful. It was a huge part of my breaking free from the painful generational patterns of regret, shame, and condemnation. I basked in His Loving-Kindness.

Reflections on Loving

Lies can make it impossible for us to forgive or to solve the many problems facing us, so let's clear them up first. So much of our resentment and shame come from lies. And remember how subtle and deceptive lies can be. Get quiet and set an intention to listen to the Spirit and not your own flesh and brain. Take a couple of deep breaths.

Ask, "Holy Spirit, what lies am I believing about myself and my life?" List every lie that He reveals.

Lies

_____

_____

_____

_____

_____

_____

_____

_____

_____

Once you have your list, take each lie and pray, "I repent for believing the lie that [speak the lie]."

Then ask, "Holy Spirit, what is the truth?" Write down the truth to replace the lie. Do this for each lie until you have gone through the entire list.

Truth

_____

_____

_____

_____

_____

_____

_____

I hope you see by now that self-forgiveness is crucial to forgiving others and gaining true freedom. Follow the example I shared in this chapter and see what Holy Spirit shows you.

Now ask, "Holy Spirit, what do I need to forgive myself for?" Write down whatever comes to you here.

_____

_____

_____

_____

_____

_____

_____

_____

Hold onto this list for now, and keep reading.

CHAPTER 17

Forgiving Others

Self-forgiveness is difficult. It requires intention and follow-through and is essential to moving on. But forgiving others . . . now we're getting to the heart of forgiveness.

When I talk of forgiving others, I'm not talking about forgiving someone for a rude look or cutting in line at the grocery store. The heart of forgiveness encompasses forgiving for the deep wounds of abuses, betrayals, and lesser offenses that build up into one giant, gaping wound. Forgiving minor infractions can be challenging, depending on how prideful, self-righteous, and controlling you are, but doing so can be a good warm-up for the more difficult places of bitterness. The deeper wounds are the ones that really blacken our hearts. When those are forgiven and released, they bring the most healing and freedom to our hearts, souls, and minds.

A powerful biblical metaphor likens humans to raw or impure gold that must be refined with fire. The refiner's fire melts all the impurities away so that only pure gold remains (Zechariah 13:9; Malachi 3:2). Pure gold is beautiful, but only after it's been refined. And if gold has a nervous system and pain receptors, the refiner's fire hurts. I know it does because I've been through that fire. They say burns are one of the most painful injuries to human flesh. The spiritual burning off all my flesh was agony, but I survived it and am better for it. And here is where I encourage you to walk through that fire too. It will transform your heart and mind, allowing compassion and grace to flow organically from you. But it takes courage, and it hurts.

If we don't forgive, it can hinder our prayers.

So many words from the Bible have challenged and encouraged me to forgive even when it felt impossible. Since I am encouraging you to do what the Bible says, let's *see* what it says.

> And when you stand praying, if you hold anything against anyone,
> forgive them, so that your Father in heaven may forgive you your sins.
> (Mark 11:25)

The idea here is that if we don't forgive, it can hinder our prayers. And if our prayers are hindered, our relationship with God is compromised. It seems like forgiveness is paramount, even above prayer. Forgive first.

> You have heard that it was said, "You shall love your neighbor
> and hate your enemy." But I [Jesus] say to you, Love your
> enemies and pray for those who persecute you.
> (Matthew 5:43–44 esv)

Then Peter came to Jesus and asked, "Lord, how many times shall I forgive my brother or sister who sins against me? Up to seven times?" Jesus answered, "I tell you, not seven times, but seventy-seven times." (Matthew 18:21–22)

Yep! We must forgive over and over and over and over. I don't think this means we allow someone to abuse us repeatedly or even stay in a relationship with someone who hurts us repeatedly without apologizing or trying to remedy or change. But there are people who are in our lives irrespective of our choices or control. In-laws, neighbors, colleagues, bosses, and even the person in line with us at Trader Joe's . . . we must bear with these people. Frankly, most people think only of themselves and offend us unintentionally. Some people struggle with jealousy and hurt us to bind up their own fears and pain. Some people misinterpret our actions or words and take offense even when we did not intend to offend, and then they retaliate. These people are often considered enemies in our lives. Countless scenarios create a repetitive offense situation. Yet we are told to forgive, even our enemies, repeatedly. So do what the Bible says.

Be kind and compassionate to one another, forgiving each other, just as in Christ God forgave you. (Ephesians 4:32)

This verse emphasizes the "walk out" of forgiveness. We must forgive from the heart, and that forgiveness looks like kindness and compassion. When I earnestly pray to forgive someone, God begins to foster compassion in me for that person. Holy Spirit reveals that this person who has wounded me has her own wounds controlling her mode of operation, and compassion grows. Organically, then, I can pray in the Spirit for her and release her of whatever debt I think she owes me. This is what transforms bitterness into kindness as I forgive from the heart.

Death to Self

Just as forgiving oneself requires identifying lies, deep forgiveness of others requires death to self. And death to self does not feel good. In fact, it's not really something you should survive. Believe me, I know. My friend gave me a book called *Let Go to Get Peace and Real Joy* by François Fénelon. He talks about this idea of death to self:

> Whatever spiritual knowledge or feelings we may have, they are all a delusion if they do not lead us to the real and constant practice of dying to self. And it is true that we do not die without suffering. Nor is it possible to be considered truly dead while there is any part of us which is yet alive. This spiritual death (which is really a blessing in disguise) is undeniably painful. It cuts swift and deep into our innermost thoughts and desires with all their parts, exposing us for what we really are. The Great Physician, who sees in us what we cannot see, knows exactly where to place the knife. He cuts away that which we are most reluctant to give up. And how it hurts! But we must remember that pain is only felt where there is life, and where there is life is just the place where death is needed.[20]

Death to self makes room for supernatural Love.

Yes, to all of that! Ho! Yes! That is what I am trying to convey. Dying to self is required for all aspects of living free. But I had not experienced it more fully at any other time than when I was endeavoring to forgive. Indeed, forgiveness can be the vehicle for a plethora of soul-cleansing deaths. Hurts and offenses that need forgiving grow roots and tentacles that produce thoughts, feelings, beliefs, and actions . . . all of which need to die. Further, many of the resulting thoughts, feelings, and actions have nothing directly to do with whatever it was that offended us. So, yeah, we gotta die.

But how can we forgive people who commit heinous acts of abuse? How can we forgive people who persecute us? How can we forgive repeated malicious acts? How can we forgive those who selfishly act in ways that tear out our hearts and trample them on the ground? That is what the Bible tells us to do. That is what Jesus does for us, and He calls us to do the same for those who have hurt us in our lives. But how?

Christian theology says that the only thing that could completely forgive humanity's sin was Jesus's death on the cross. He had to die. And not just some simple "natural" death. His was a tortuous, unjustified, punishing execution in full view of a mocking crowd! Many who do not believe in Jesus or the Bible have taken issue with this aspect of Christian belief, and I don't blame them. It seems so backward and unloving that God the Father would send His only Son to earth to die such a disgusting death because that heinous execution would be the only thing that could usher in forgiveness for our sins.

Theologians have written countless books on the subject. I've read a few. I'm not sure they would convince my questioning friends. All I know is that forgiveness often feels like a torturous death. Some of the things I forgave required me to die a painful death to self, pride, fear, entitlement, and self-will . . . death to all of my flesh and every dark spirit with which I had prospered.

If you were to ask me to identify only *one* thing that ushered in freedom for me, I couldn't do it. There are two. The first is supernatural Love, the reason why I titled this final section "Loving." The second is death to self. I'm not kidding. Death to self makes room for supernatural Love. My flesh did not have space for God's supernatural Love. It was bogged down with bitterness, pride, and all the tag-a-longs of unforgiveness. My ego—my "flesh"—had to die to make room for God's Love.

So, this is the launching pad for forgiving others. I have learned that death is an ongoing process for the Christian. Paul said, "I die every day" (1 Corinthians 15:31 ESV). I think he's talking about our choice to put to death the things of the flesh to live abundantly in Christ. Jesus wants to give us His fullness and total intimacy with Him, which is almost impossible to imagine. But I have glimpsed it, and it is sweeter than anything here on earth. It is sweeter than anything I could possibly conjure in my little mind. And it came through the death of Rena.

Walking Out Forgiveness: Steven

I like the version of the Lord's Prayer that says, "Forgive us our debts, as we forgive our debtors" (Matthew 6:12 NKJV). The language of debt resonates with me because when someone hurts me or sins against me, they steal from me. They have taken something from me. If someone molests a child, they steal their innocence. If someone physically abuses you, they steal your health and sense of safety. If someone gossips about you, they steal a part of your community and reputation.

Everything requiring forgiveness can be seen in the light of having something taken from you. Even if someone flips me off on the freeway because I cut them off inadvertently, it steals my joy for that second. I may feel hurt or offended, and that sense of well-being and peace I was experiencing the second before the finger gesture is now gone—taken from me. Unless I forgive them, they may continue to take up my headspace until my next human interaction. And even then, I may talk about the person who flipped me off.

Throughout my daughter's dating relationship with Steven, there were many offenses. We did not handle all of this perfectly, but we did try. I think they tried too. But I'm telling my side, so I will just do that. We attempted to mentor Steven to some degree because we knew he had no role models or teaching about Christian dating and pursuing a young woman with honor. We met with him several times. Unfortunately, several of those meetings were him apologizing for some infraction against our standards. It felt like every promise he made, he broke. And he broke them pretty royally.

I don't think even he would argue that point. I'm not saying we did not see any effort from him, and I'm not saying Amanda did not egg him on. She had a part in all of it. Still, it was sorely disappointing. It taught us not to trust his word at all, which was yet another huge red flag to us. Although we were impressed that he would come to us and apologize, it became clear that he hadn't changed his behavior, kinda like me trying to change but not having any power to change.

After a while, we quit believing him, and he quit seeking us. At that point, he just pursued Amanda, and I had a sinking feeling that we were now the bad guys, and he was going to win our daughter. He fought for her, and he won. This happened in painful bits involving the entire life plan she'd had before he came along. Each time a big or little piece of this revealed itself, it crushed me. It felt like a powerful set of big waves crashing so fast that I could hardly catch my breath, only to look and see a tidal wave on the horizon. I'm not a strong swimmer. The ocean intimidates me.

I practiced taking each wave with a forgiveness prayer. "I choose to forgive Steven for . . ." whatever I found out that day. I think they thought they weren't doing anything wrong most of the time. But I was in the middle of the set and could see the tidal wave. So sometimes underwater and sometimes gasping for air, I would pray, drowning in my own tears.

I walked out this forgiveness by praying for him and taking my ugly, fearful thoughts captive, repenting for partnering with fear and asking for more faith, and praying day and night. That's a pretty extensive forgiveness walkout. It includes just about every tenet of walking out the Christian faith. Love your enemies? Check. (Matthew 5:44) Trust God? Check. (Proverbs 3:5) Do not fear for I [God] am with you? Check. (Isaiah 41:10) Pray for those who persecute you? Check. (Matthew 5:44) Do not be anxious about anything? Check. (Philippians 4:6) Forgive from the heart? Check. (Matthew 18:35) Love bears all things? Check. (1 Corinthians 13:7) Be humble? Check. (Ephesians 4:2) Jesus is the way? Check. (John 14:6)

So when Steven flew to Colorado, where our daughter was attending college, packed up her car with all of her things and moved her back to California into his shack—clearly against all of our wishes, clearly not caring about our relationship with him or Amanda—we were beyond hurt and angry. We had invested nineteen years of everything we had into this girl. To us, he had taken every privilege from her and placed her in poverty and danger without a single regard for her best interest or ours. To us, he seemed to go for what he wanted alone. I can start fuming just thinking about it. The offense was so deep. I called Barb.

"Are you ready to forgive him?" she asked. I knew I had to. She had been walking me through transformation, "to work out [my] salvation with fear and trembling" (Philippians 2:12). But from my perspective, this man had literally stolen our daughter from us. He had mocked my every effort to give my daughter more than I had been given and had convinced her that my priorities were off-base. "Forgive him? No, I'd like to kill him quickly and get rid of the body so I'd never have to see it again. Wipe it out of existence. That's what I want to do."

But, by this point, I had a lot of experience with self-death in forgiving Steven. All of that practice was preparation for an even more difficult forgiveness walk-out. I had experienced how hard it was to forgive, and that experience strengthened my ability to forgive more. So I started to pray forgiveness.

Death to Rena

The Bible clearly states, and Jesus clearly demonstrated, that we are to love everybody all the time. Love is not something we do because we feel like it. That's just expressing fondness. True and biblical love is acting lovingly no matter how you feel—even and especially when you are hurt, angry, or offended.

Heidi Baker often says, "Love looks like something." Yes, it does. It looks like literally laying down our lives for others . . . laying down our opinions, our politics, our narratives about the relationship . . . laying down every part of our flesh. And oh, the death of self that occurs when we allow the Holy Spirit to change our hearts and we walk out that change. He will soften our hearts and give us supernatural Love, but if we don't walk that out, our hearts will turn to stone again.

So, I'm lecturing too long without sharing how this happened to me. I want to take you back to the beginning of this section on forgiveness, back when I was in a region of captivity in chains to fear, self-pity, anger, and hopelessness. I had been calling Barb and ranting about the turmoil I was experiencing. Basically, I had partnered with some hateful, fearful spirit and allowed it to take up residence in my heart and mind. Therefore, what came forth from my mouth was bitter, hateful, and fear-filled.

I was lamenting over my fear regarding Amanda's future and her children's future. I was blaming Steven for subjecting my daughter and grandchildren to this supposed future. I knew better than to spew this poison onto most people in my life, especially my husband. To him, I think I looked deeply troubled. The only person I could freely talk with was Barb. So I did. And I did. And I did. One day, she said she would no longer listen to me. She told me that I was full of hatred, judgment, and fear, and that listening to me day after day was hurting her spirit.

"I know! That's why I'm telling you! I'm stuck! I need help!" Was she not listening?

"Well, Rena," she replied, "you're going to have to forgive him and move on to loving him. He's your son-in-law. The Lord has allowed that. So you can either stay in hatred and judgment or start bringing Kingdom."

"What if he abuses her? Do I have to forgive him and love him then? What if he abuses my grandchildren?" I whined.

"Rena, I'm not giving you my opinion. I'm telling you what the Word says. It says to love no matter what, forgive and not keep records of wrong, and always hope. I'm telling you what Jesus did, and you already know this."

I hated what she was saying. I didn't want to do any of this. Mostly though, it just felt impossible.

"So you're saying I have to forgive Steven for stealing my daughter's future and whatever he's subjecting her to? I can't do it, Barbara," I said with tears. "That's why I keep reaching out to you!"

"I know you can't," she said softly. "But you have to lay it all down and let Jesus do it."

"I can't lay it down. It's too precious." I felt so lost and alone.

Too precious. Isn't it strange how bitterness and hatred can be precious to us? We hold onto unforgiveness like some sort of pride trophy. "That person is so bad. I treasure my bitter hatred and unforgiveness toward him. I don't care if it ruins family relationships, or holidays, or gives me cancer. [I'm not blaming cancer patients for their illnesses. I'm acknowledging that bitterness can manifest in physical illness.] It's so precious to me; I will die preserving it." We don't say that aloud, but actions speak louder than words. Look around. Look inside. We hold others' offenses against us as precious. Yuk.

"Ok, well, I can't hear it anymore. So, call me when you're ready." And that was Barbara's final word to me.

I was so pathetic. I was so hurt and angry with Barb at that point. I knew she was right . . . sort of. But surely she must not be understanding my internal torture! I felt totally abandoned by her. In fact, when I finally called her back and told her I was ready to lay myself aside and try to forgive Steven, I wanted her first to apologize for abandoning me. She really wouldn't do that. She said she was sorry I was hurt, but she maintained that she had not wronged me and had nothing to repent for. Come to think of it, I don't think I ever apologized for spewing all over her for all those weeks. Sorry, Barb. Truly, I am sorry. That must have been difficult to bear. Thank you for putting up with me as long as you did.

Barbara knew I would need to lay some foundation before I could truly forgive Steven. The process she took me through was inspired by Holy Spirit, who knew my soul was wounded and needed some attention before I could release Steven because forgiving him involved so many aspects of my heart and mind. My hopes and dreams as a mother, my prayers, my failures, my own darkness, old soul wounds—they were all caught up in a tangled mess inside me. She asked me to write a letter to God telling Him how I see Him. I've reproduced it below. Notice how it reflects the lies I was believing.

Letter to God:

God, I'm so afraid of You. You have allowed such pain, and I think You'll continue to do so. You have taken my daughter, and I don't think You'll ever return her. I know You could fix our relationship, but You won't. I have been a terrible mother to her. Even now, I won't speak to her husband, and it hurts her every day. I am a terrible mother. Sarah is dead.[21] We had a tight bond. Therapists aren't supposed to love their clients, but I loved her, and she loved me. I was a surrogate mother figure to her. No amount of good intentions or love from me was enough to help. In the end, I think she felt I didn't love her, and I think my daughter feels the same. How else could Steven convince her, or she feels that her home suppressed her, that we don't believe in her, or that Jeff is scary and always tries to trick her? How else could she reject us fully for a wolf? I know You hate me, God, and want to kill me. I hate me. I know if I let You kill me, I will be better. But I'm afraid You'll do it over and over and make me watch Steven abuse my daughter and grandchildren, all the while telling me to love and forgive him. I'll fail. I can't do that. How can You force me to watch that? I can't keep my eyes on You while my daughter is in danger. I trust You to take care of her, but she won't listen to You. You told her what to do, and she ignored You for Steven. Are You helpless too? Who are You? I have no peace anymore.

I texted a picture of my journal entry to Barb. She responded right away with a follow-up assignment. She told me to ask Father God how He sees me. I wrote this the same hour I wrote the above.

How do you see me, Father God?

Rena, I see you as lost, scared, and alone. I see you with your back turned to Me as I keep asking you to come to Me. You keep saying no. I see you as angry. I see you as a loving mother who did her very best and more. I saw you learning all you could from good mothers so you could give your children all they needed. You are a serious mother who took the job seriously and wanted to please Me because I blessed you with three beautiful children. You dedicated them to Me and faithfully taught them My Word. I saw you working hard and being disciplined to read the Bible every day to your family. I loved that you did that. I loved your heart when it was touched and excited and convicted every day by My words and how you talked about that with your children. I see you as listening too much to judgment from demons . . . mostly on yourself. I have always wanted to free you from all of that. I see you are stuck there now. I see you as a powerful worker for me. If you will surrender . . . I love you. You are My daughter. Please don't reject Me as Amanda has rejected her father. Please don't believe lies about Me as Amanda has about her father. I feel sad and hurt when you reject Me. Please don't misunderstand losses in your life as punishment from Me.

Our Father in heaven loves us so deeply and unconditionally. He's gentle and kind and always sees our best, even at our worst. I was a goner. I could no longer resist the total love of God that forgets my transgressions and remembers my best efforts even as I am cursing Him. Who else does that? Well, I wanted to. His easy forgiveness drew me to Him. I still felt hurt and hatred, but I was ready to surrender those to God.

After soaking in my restored connection with Jesus for a few weeks, I was ready to move forward with forgiving Steven. Notice that it took a few weeks. I knew how ambivalent I was about forgiving Steven and allowing myself to die. I wanted my forgiveness to be authentic and from the heart. So I soaked in the truth of my connection with God for a while to cut through the resistance inside of me.

Once I was ready to surrender, Barb suggested I must first address the lies I'd believed right after Amanda married Steven. I needed truth in my heart and mind to get free from the terrible bondage I was in. Those lies are listed in the previous chapter under the heading "Believing Lies." Feel free to look back at them with this context in mind.

Five days after replacing those lies with the truth during a quiet time with Jesus, Holy Spirit prompted me to write down all that the Lord had shown me since Amanda began to rebel. I did, and I titled it "Things God Has Shown Me Over the Last Two Years." Looking back, I see that this was a faith-building exercise. Holy Spirit knew I needed to remember that I had the gift of faith, and for good reason.

Things God has shown me:

He has a beautiful plan for Steven's life. He has reconciliation for Jasmine[22] and Steven.

He wants Steven to love and care for Jasmine as the honored mother of his son.

He wants to redeem Steven and his entire sphere of influence.

He loves Steven and sees the beauty in his heart.

He has had me pray in earnest for all of this to come to fruition.

He wants us to love and embrace Steven as he strives for transformation and sanctification as a new believer.

I am to pray for sincere repentance and that Jesus would be the only Lord of his life.

I am to repent, forgive, and love no matter what.

I am not owed anything from Steven or Amanda.

I am to pray that they honor God alone.

I am nothing, and their honor to me is only a product of honoring God. It has nothing to do with me.

I am to wait until the Lord shows me what to do.

God is using Amanda's life to better Franklin's life.

I am to trust God with Amanda's life.

I am to look only to God and trust Him.

I am full of ugly, sinful blackness, and my only hope is God!

The Day I Forgave Steven

Barbara said it was okay if I could not forgive Steven. All I had to do was be *willing* to forgive and let Holy Spirit do the work. I had taken essential steps that laid the groundwork for me to forgive. Notice that this was a process. Having laid down some foundation, we set a date and time to pray through it. We got together on the phone. I went into a quiet room in my house and closed the door. She simply told me to start. "Holy Spirit, I choose to forgive Steven for . . ." I listed everything I could think of each time, repeating, "I choose to forgive Steven for . . ."

There is something powerful about repeating those words. The declaration seems to take prominence over the offense I'm forgiving, and I'm reminded each time that *the choice to forgive* is more powerful than *the things I'm choosing to forgive.* Do not underestimate the will and the power of intention. By saying, "I choose," I'm engaging my will and thereby setting the intention to forgive. Forgiveness has not yet happened, but just the intention to forgive gets you halfway there, at least.

Even so, the words did not come easily. I was like the two-year-old who just smacked someone, and is being ordered to say she's sorry. I didn't want to forgive. I still felt I was in the right. The loss was still there, big time. Nothing had been repaired. But I knew my heart needed to be cleaned out and filled with Love, and I knew Jesus was my only hope for this miracle. So, I prayed to forgive through bitter, painful, pathetic tears. I chose as an act of my will to forgive.

As I declared my choice to forgive, the room began to feel more like a scene from *The Exorcist.* Okay, not really. There was no green puke spewing across the room, the bed didn't levitate, and demonic voices didn't hurl profanity at me. But I did begin to heave and grabbed a trash can to catch the contents of my stomach. My body was writhing, and I curled up on the floor, feeling beaten down and exhausted.

So minus the dramatic license and special effects, I was clearly experiencing a spiritual battle for my soul. I could see myself in the spirit. I was stuck in a pit, chained up, my arms in shackles. It was a deep pit, and wolf-like creatures were guarding and tormenting me with threats and lies. I could hear them saying my prayers wouldn't work. They chanted lies about Amanda's future and her children's future. They were super scary and mean.

I saw a clear picture of what I had been experiencing. It was a movie about my emotions. No wonder I had been in such agony. I reported what I saw, and Barbara encouraged me to look for Jesus as she prayed over me. I was so tired and afraid. I couldn't see Jesus anywhere. He was not there with me.

Intuitively, I knew just to say His name. I began to repeat, "Jesus, Jesus, Jesus . . ." As I continued to say His name, I began to see Him. He came down into that pit, took off the shackles, and freed me from the chains. He carried me out of the pit and set me down on the earth. I felt His love and compassion around and inside me. I told Barbara what was happening, and we knew it was true. It was more true than the physical room I was inhabiting.

Concluding Thoughts on Forgiveness

The apostle Paul once told a man who tried to buy the miraculous power of the Holy Spirit with money that he could not receive the gift of the Holy Spirit. The reason he gave the man was, "For I see that you are full of bitterness and captive to sin" (Acts 8:23).

That was me. Filled with bitter bile secretions puking up nasty thoughts and words every waking hour. I spent weeks trapped—chained to hatred, unforgiveness, and fear. It was complete agony. I really believed there was no way out for me. You can see it plain as day when you read the lies I believed:

> *It can never be fixed.*
>
> *No matter what, there's no answer.*
>
> *I'm totally trapped.*

By following Barb's instructions to ask Holy Spirit about the lies I was believing, openly telling Father God how I was feeling (rather than staying locked up in those feelings), and hearing from Him about how He sees me, I turned my focus upward and was able to forgive myself. The ability to forgive is like a muscle that needs reps at lower weights to work up to heavy lifting. I'd practiced forgiving others for smaller things over the previous three years. That practice kept me walking close to the Spirit because forgiveness is not a natural tendency. Once I was willing to adjust my focus, challenge the lies, and die to every bit of self, I could repent and forgive Steven.

If you think about it, forgiveness is the foundation. How did Jesus heal people? He forgave them. How did Jesus rescue us from the clutches of the enemy? Yes, He died on the cross as a sacrifice for our iniquity. But that grace is a product of His forgiveness. Even on the cross, as they crucified Him, jeering and celebrating His torturous death, He said, "Father, forgive them, for they know not what they do" (Luke 23:34 ESV).

If God sets us free by forgiving us, then we must forgive others. And don't forget, God forgives everyone for everything. There are no exceptions.

Reflections on Loving

Forgiving from the heart is a type of heart transplant, and it doesn't happen without death to self. This abridged version of a forgiveness prayer in five parts is a start. If you want to go further, please reference this chapter, spend time with Holy Spirit, and forgive more.

Step 1

Ask, "Holy Spirit, who do I need to forgive?"

List the names that come to mind.

(If you answered this question about yourself in the chapter 16 reflections, you could use that list now and forgive yourself.)

Step 2

Choose one name from your list above and ask, "Holy Spirit, what do I need to forgive_____for?"

Write, "I choose to forgive_____for_____." Keep repeating this phrase until you have listed every offense. As you do this, stay meditative and listen for Holy Spirit's words.

Step 3

Ask, "Holy Spirit, show me my part."

Now allow Holy Spirit to show you how you have contributed to the offenses and brokenness around you. Then list each thing you are shown or sense, repeating this phrase, "I repent for_____."

Step 4

Ask, "Holy Spirit, what does_____need to be blessed with?"

Now list every blessing you sense in the spirit. Be sure it's not your flesh. A clue would be if the "blessing" reflects anything controlling or critical, like "I bless_____with not being selfish."

A blessing is a free gift from God, so bless by repeating this phrase, "I bless _____with_____."

Step 5

Once you've completed praying blessings, pray this way:

"I release _____of all debt owed to me. I give _____ to you, Father, to teach, to discipline, and to love.

And I choose to forgive _____fully from the heart in accordance with Your will."

~ Amen

CHAPTER 18

Humility

The day I forgave Steven—the one when I was taken out of hell where the enemy had been holding me for several weeks after the wedding—I began to love Steven supernaturally. The love was deposited into my heart as a part of that deliverance. It came as I cried aloud, "Jesus, Jesus, Jesus . . ." Remember how His name was all I could say? I was lifted out of despair and began to see Steven in a loving light until I felt supernatural love for him.

I knew I needed to walk out this love, so I continued to press into Holy Spirit, asking how I might do that. As I brought my relationship with Steven before the Father, He prompted me to seek Steven's forgiveness. "You gotta be kidding me," was my first thought. And the second was, "Yep, sounds like Holy Spirit." And I knew it was righteous.

By this time, I understood that the Lord's completed work in me was going to require utter humility and, in a sense, no trace of the self in me. I was going to die. He was going to kill me completely. And what better way to do that than to humble me before Steven? Naturally, I avoided meeting with Holy Spirit about it for a week or more. Finally, I sat down and prayed this prayer: "Lord, please show me if, when, and how to address Steven. Please show me, Jesus, what obedience to Your Love looks like."

He did not answer me directly at first. Instead, I heard Him answer, "Strength is in Christ's Love. Truth is in Christ's Love. Grace is in Christ's Love." I've learned that when this happens, God often has a larger precept He wants to teach me. Each time this happens, I slow down to receive each answer while continuing to press in for more of whatever He has.

I just say, "Yes, and please show me more." So, on that day, I said, "Yes. Thank you, Holy Spirit. I want to walk in the Truth, Strength, and Grace of Your Love, Jesus."

And then Holy Spirit began to give me words of repentance as He gently showed me myself. I continued in my prayer. "I repent for any scrap or obstacle of pride in this situation. I renounce all pride in my heart, Lord, and I bind my heart to Yours, Jesus. Give me Your humble heart."

Sometimes, the Holy Spirit puts words of Scripture in my mouth as I'm praying. I love it when that happens. That day I prayed from Psalm 86:11, "Teach me your ways, O Lord," I said. "Give me an undivided heart so I may walk in Your ways."

I continued this prayer by asking specifically, like Holy Spirit was my therapist, "So, do I just call him up and meet him at a park and say something like, 'I've asked you here to repent to you for the wrongs I have trespassed against you? I ask that you hear me and let me know if there's anything else?'"

And then Holy Spirit showed me what to say. He let me practice repenting in my prayer. It went like this:

> *Steven, I repent to you for rejecting you from the beginning for Amanda. I repent to you for responding to your oppression rather than God's image in you. I repent to you for not consistently showing Christ's Love. I repent to you for speaking to family and friends negatively about you. I repent to you for not blessing your marriage. I repent to you for not being gracious to your mother at our first meeting. I love you, and I receive you as a son.*

That was it. Clear and concise, yet, oh, so humble. Should I say here why I thought I did not owe him an apology? Should I recite the long list of why I believed he owed me an apology and for what? Absolutely not! I did everything listed above. And those things were in direct violation of God's commandments to love, forgive, and trust in Him. Therefore, I needed to repent without a single "but."

Repenting Heals Hurts

The day I repented to Steven, we met in a park near his house. It was a short meeting. He just listened as I read exactly what Holy Spirit told me to say. It seemed a bit emotional for him as I admitted those things to him. I think it's because Holy Spirit had me repent for the core hurts he had experienced from me.

As a therapist, I know how healing it is to have someone understand and verbalize how they have hurt you. Conversely, I also know how damaging it can be when an emotional wound is never seen, understood, and validated. Spiritually speaking, I was not surprised but was struck with how powerful it has been when I simply acknowledge to another person that I understand I have hurt them and how.

When I go to Holy Spirit and ask Him to show me how I need to repent to someone, He shows me specifically and accurately how to address how my actions have hurt the other person. Trust me; it's way better than me thinking about what I've done. I get in the way and start making excuses in my mind or focusing on how they have hurt me as well. Then I have to take those thoughts captive and pray a blessing on the person, and it can be an unproductive circle. It's so much better just to lay myself before the Lord and ask Him. He answers. That way, I can give the other person exactly what they need to hear from me to heal their hearts.

You'd have to ask Steven how that whole experience was for him. I think he was scratching his head for a while afterward. I'm sure he wondered how this woman, who had been very clear and vocal about how he was wrong and bad for her daughter, had suddenly repented and received him as a son. He would wait and see. It's been over five years now, and I think he knows I meant it. I think he has seen the fruit of my words by the power of the Holy Spirit at work in me. At least, I hope so.

For my part, it was a victory—a huge victory! I did not want to do it. The devil constantly whispered in my ear that I should judge and reject Steven. He still tries to get me to do that. Since that day, things have transpired that tempted me to do so, but I choose to love on the Lord's side. I say, "Get behind me, Satan," and I am victorious over the schemes of the devil.

So I say, all praise to the Glorious Father of Light. He has set me free from hate and bitterness and judgment and pride. Thank You, God. It is not me. I cannot boast. But God . . . Victory.

God Is the Only Right One

I'm now walking with a woman as Barbara walked with me. She is a sharp and successful woman. She agrees with my husband that there are only solutions when facing a problem! She's brilliant at coming up with creative and powerful solutions to her problems and the many people who come to her for help. Recently, she got a powerful word from the Lord. He said, "What do you know?" I love how when we hear from Holy Spirit. It's often so conversational and brief. He sends zingers. God is not verbose, in my experience, anyway.

This was one of those times—those four little words said it all. They hit her right between the eyes because she sees situations clearly and has a lot of good answers. But the Lord's word to her was, "What do you know?" We laughed at the irony of her human efforts in the face of this powerful word. God loves irony. I do, too, because it's so smart and makes me laugh.

I love to laugh. Don't you? I used to be so serious. One unexpected and fun benefit of breaking free from so much bondage is that I got my laugh back. One day, I was laughing at something silly, and it hit me—I was laughing! Maybe I noticed it because I had not laughed heartily in so long. Now I have a loud, obnoxious cackle of a laugh. I don't care, though. It's deep and real. Sometimes in our pride, we take things so seriously and tackle every obstacle with a vengeance. Humility counteracts striving and is altogether more fun.

So, if we keep quiet and press into Holy Spirit for direction in our lives, if we recognize that we do not know, if we stay quiet even when we think we know, if we wait for clear direction, and even then, if we don't blab about it, and if we just do what He says, then we are getting the idea of Humility. There are a lot of "ifs" there, I know. I wrote it this way to show the many ways we begin to insert ourselves or our agendas and try to do it ourselves rather than letting Holy Spirit lead us.

Shortly after my daughter became engaged to Steven, I was once again on my face crying out for God to stop this marriage. My forehead was pressed against the hardwood flooring in my living room, and my body was curled into yoga's child's pose as I pleaded with God through tears (which was commonplace for me during this season) for Amanda and Steven to "honor us," "to honor their father and their mother." There I was, quoting Scripture to God and feeling quite assured that this prayer was in alignment with His will. I was sure my prayer was being heard with mercy and compassion from above and that His angels were working on my behalf.

And then the Father said, "You don't deserve honor."

I stopped breathing for a second to consider the clear word I was receiving. The Bible tells us to honor our father and mother. That's all I was praying for . . . yet this word felt like the Lord disapproved of my prayer. I kept my head pressed against that floor. "What?"

"You don't deserve honor," He repeated.

And then a revelation came to me. I instantly knew that my prayer was a prideful prayer born out of embarrassment, humiliation, fear, and pain. I saw the prideful root of my prayer. God showed me that I was trying to be a lord in Steven and Amanda's lives. That was a zinger. Here I'd thought I was earnestly crying out to God for my daughter. Yikes.

And then I sensed another zinger. "You pray for them to honor Me."

Still with my head on the ground, I began to pray this way, "I repent for trying to take Your place as lord in their lives. I give them to You and trust You with their future. Please, Lord, I ask that Amanda and Steven honor You . . ."

It was so profound for me. I completely transformed my prayer life at that moment. I can't say I liked that revelation or understanding. But it did humble me a little more. And I knew it was true and righteous.

God is the only One who is right. We can think we are right. We can find Bible verses that we think prove our point. But such arguments come from pride in the heart, which boasts, "I am right, and you are wrong."

God is the only right One. "What do you know?" "You don't deserve honor!"

Low and Slow

Slowing down is a vital part of humility. I often say to myself, "low and slow." Low reminds me to be humble, and slowing down is one method of interrupting the temptation to act in pride. Keeping this posture enables us to hear from God and walk by the Spirit.

There's a quote from François Fénelon that isn't about me, but it surely applies.

> Few people had an experience more fitting to humiliate the heart and destroy self-confidence. The good that comes from any experience of personal weakness is the realization that God wants us to be lowly and obedient. So may the Lord keep you.[23]

It cut deeply to know people were gossiping about and judging my daughter and my parenting. It was humiliating when certain aspects of the situation were coarsely displayed in front of my community. My self-confidence as a mother was in tatters. Every weakness seemed to be on display in full color. I felt humiliated. But it was good for me.

Only after the destruction of Rena did I surrender to God fully. It's like Alcoholics Anonymous (AA) says: you have to hit rock bottom. I think I hit rock bottom about once a week in different ways. Sometimes I was humiliated by some decision or happening involving Amanda. Other times, I was hurt by others' gossip and judgment of me and/or my daughter. Often, my own ugly thoughts were horrifying and humiliating. And too often, all of these things were happening simultaneously. It was a prolonged, chronic kind of humiliation that gradually, bit by bit, took out my legs entirely until I was on the ground, shattered, reaching for the One, the only One who knows.

He said, "Stay down. Low and slow. Stay low." As if the goal itself is to be lowly! Indeed, I think it is.

Low and slow. I'm having necklaces made with those words. That's how profound the idea is to me. I do not mess around where jewelry is concerned.

In obedience, I stayed low because, frankly, I had no better ideas. (Thank the Lord, or I might have tried one, and it most definitely would have failed.) That looked like saying almost nothing, doing absolutely nothing by my flesh, taking my solicitations, grief, and pain to Jesus (multiple times daily), and waiting for Holy Spirit to direct me. Low and slow. I did not move until I was sure Holy Spirit was directing me. I just prayed and waited.

The waiting periods were bittersweet. The Lord was so merciful to show me my mindsets and behaviors that were out of line as He offered His hand to show me a better way. It's very simple, really, even though we usually do not do it. He showed me to live as if I did not know better (humility), to consider all others better than myself (humility), and to treat all people, no matter what they had done, with honor (humility).

I knew it was right and that it did not come from me. I allowed these lessons to sink in as I languished on the ground day after day. And in that broken state, soaking in these truths, my mind was renewed. I received a new heart—not one of stone but of flesh. That new heart began to beat strongly, and these truths of humility pulsed through my arteries, giving life to the lessons on humility.

I am so thankful because the person I used to be looked good on the outside, and there was good in me. But there was serious garbage mixed in with the good.

Humility Leads to Compassion

Repenting to Steven was a culmination of the work God had done in me to humble me. It was a manifestation of humility to go to the person I felt most wronged by and repent to him. I'm sure Steven also felt wronged, so it did not seem so strange. Perhaps it was validating to him. But for me and others close to me, it seemed pretty upside-down. God loves to turn things on their head. I had no doubt about that when He said, "You don't deserve honor."

One of the things that stands out so starkly is how much compassion I gained for Steven. When we met, this guy was in his mid-to-late twenties with a two-year-old boy he absolutely adored, born out of wedlock. He had failed to make it work with the boy's mother. His past was littered with bad choices and many dire consequences. But he sincerely wanted to do better for himself and his son. Who could blame him for being taken with Amanda? She was beautiful, sweet, and encouraging, and she spoke life into his future. And he did try to go about it in a new and better way. He asked Jeff if he could date Amanda, but Jeff said no. (Who could blame him? Amanda was eighteen, still in high school, etc.) What was Steven to do? He really believed Amanda was the one. He wanted to build a life with her, not take advantage of her youth and naïvety. His heart was for good for his future.

I remember talking to him one day after he'd crossed a boundary Jeff and I had set. In a vulnerable moment, I asked him, "Are you going to take my daughter away from us?"

"I don't want to," he replied.

Ultimately, they did marry without our blessing, but I don't believe he wanted it to go that way. So as great a loss as it was for us, he lost out too. And there were many similar examples of how Steven lost out or was hurt. As the Lord showed me my part in hurting Steven, I began to understand where he stood. I was surprised to notice compassion toward him growing in my heart. Yes, there were many mistakes along the way, but he was a man in love. What else can I say? Compassion.

It's the same with every person. It's the same with my family. It's the same with your family. We are all broken and lost and doing the best we can. Freedom comes when we let go of our judgment on those who hurt us, allow ourselves to be humbled, repent for our part, and receive compassion and love toward those who hurt us. Then we pass compassion and love on to future generations.

Humility Draws Us Closer

It's important to note that I did not repent to Steven to fix things between Steven and me. Every relationship on earth is a reflection of my relationship with God. I repented to Steven in pursuit of a closer relationship with God. My relationship with the Father, with Jesus, and with Holy Spirit is of utmost importance to me, and while it may seem like I don't care about others, that's not true. This is another profound paradox of relationship with God.

When Jesus was on earth, the religious leaders of His time asked Him what was the greatest of the commandments. There are 613 commandments in all, so this was a big question. Jesus replied,

> "'Love the Lord your God with all your heart and with all your soul and with all your mind.' This is the first and greatest commandment.

And the second is like it: 'Love your neighbor as yourself.' All the Law and the Prophets hang on these two commandments." (Matthew 22:37–40)

For me, forgiving others and repentance to others is obedience to the first command more than it is to the second.

When I seek intimacy with God, He shows me how I haven't loved others well. When I repent and take action to love others well, I am drawn closer to God. It's this beautiful circle. And this focus is not without benefit to others. I see that it takes the pressure off them. I used to need affirmation, fairness, and connection with others pretty desperately. Now, I could care less, yet my relationships with others have become healthier and richer. God is a beautiful mystery, and He is all we need. Once we realize this, everything else comes to us.

Humility releases the process and the results here on earth to God alone. We quit striving, controlling, and judging as if we have any control and could possibly know best in any real eternal way. Total death to self means surrendering all, even the most precious parts of our lives. Yes, even our children. That was my final lesson.

Reflections on Loving

Death to self. Low and slow. God is the only right One. Repent to others even when you feel right. Humility is good. You might want to skip this reflection at first. Or you could be eager to rid yourself of yourself. Just try it. You got this!

1. Describe a time in your life when you felt humiliated.

_____

_____

_____

_____

_____

_____

_____

2. Reflecting on that time, how was it a good thing?

_____

_____

_____

_____

_____

_____

3. Is there a situation in your life today that provides an opportunity to be humble rather than right? If so, describe that situation here.

_____

_____

_____

_____

_____

_____

_____

_____

_____

_____

_____

_____

CHAPTER 19

Sovereignty, the Final Lesson

*P*aradox fascinates me. So much in life and faith is paradoxical. A quick Google search defines it as "a statement or proposition that, despite sound [or apparently sound] reasoning from acceptable premises, leads to a conclusion that seems senseless, logically unacceptable, or self-contradictory."[24] I like paradox because it boggles the mind. It reminds me of how limited my understanding is. I find comfort in the fact that logic and reason fall gravely short in determining and deciphering the truth. The point of paradox requires faith for understanding, and even still, we cannot quite understand. So we must reach for greatness by surrendering all we think we know.

I want to define sovereignty clearly, so you know what I am discussing here. To say God is sovereign refers to "God's exercise of power over his creation."[25] Sovereignty basically means that God is in control of all things, and they all conform to His will.

God's sovereignty is paradoxical to me in a couple of obvious ways. First, how can God be sovereign when so much of life and the world is clearly out of control? Can a good God be in control in a seemingly out-of-control world? The second paradox of God's sovereignty is more personal to me. It's hard to explain, and it feels like a rock in my core . . . not a good rock. It's more like a heavy lump deep inside.

This second paradox of His sovereignty is that almost everything I know, practice, and experience about God often seems utterly meaningless when I most need to stand upon it. The promises of the Bible have seemed meaningless when I needed them most. Promises about how God will give you whatever you ask for (Mark 11:24; John 11:22; 1 John 5:14–15) just boggle my mind. I'm supposed to believe and stand in faith, but these promises are meaningless in the face of God's sovereignty, and so, actually, I am called to surrender all to God because He is sovereign. Such a difficult paradox. One that I do not like when it's happening to me.

When I was a little girl, I knew things were very awry in my home. I saw many in my family lying to themselves about the functionality of their lives, trying to act like everything was fine, only to explode or fall apart intermittently because so much was severely out of order. I knew it was wrong, whether it was verbal, physical, substance abuse, or just the tolerance of any of the above. Not wrong in a moral sense, although that is probably true too. But, wrong, like *deep-inside* wrong, like not good for thriving and growing. Bad-for-the-soul wrong. Four-year-old Rena could easily discern that. And she wanted beauty and growth and strength and love that conquers all that wrong stuff.

And my family did have love. Real love that forgives and cares and takes care of each other. I knew what love felt like. I was blessed with many people who loved me dearly and protected me from abuse. I thank God for those people and how they taught me about love.

Unfortunately, there was so much brokenness. I needed something more to break through all the dysfunction. I looked to television for examples, but *Leave It to Beaver* doesn't even begin to address the complexities that I was dealt. I was left longing for something I had no practical idea how to attain.

So, I floundered for a while, as I've detailed in the earlier chapters.

My story doesn't seem like the story of a good God in control. But God is sovereign, and He chose this family and this life for me.

Trying to Be Sovereign

Finally, I gave up on my family of origin and set out to create my own family. I would give my daughter everything I longed for as a little girl. I did not do this perfectly. Of course, I didn't. Amanda has graciously informed me of the many ways I have let her down. And she is right about those things. That's her book. I was very intentional in creating a beautiful life and family. I did my best . . . just as my mom did.

Doing all these "right" things gave me a false sense of security. I sort of thought I was sovereign and in control. I believed in myself more than I believed in God. As the sovereign of my little family, I guided my children, especially Amanda. I believed my efforts and the life I had created were the keys to breaking away from the painful generational patterns of my family line. But Proverbs 16 has something to say about humans and God's sovereignty.

All a person's ways seem pure to them, but
motives are weighed by the LORD.
(Proverbs 16:2)

In their hearts humans plan their course, but
the LORD establishes their steps.
(Proverbs 16:9)

I did a good job as a mom. I did a better job than my mother in many ways, but my motives weren't always the purest. Fear, unforgiveness, and judgment were mixed in with the higher motives of my heart. Fear that my children would not be okay if I didn't create a certain life for them. Unforgiveness toward my mother and others in my family caused me to judge them and anyone like them. I worked hard to keep my children safe from any such exposures. I hovered over them, controlling every aspect of their lives.

I thought my plan would work . . . whatever that meant. I really hoped it would mean my children would make good choices, be emotionally and spiritually healthy, avoid self-destructive feelings and behaviors, live fulfilled lives, work in their giftings, marry someone I loved, and be better parents than I was.

You know, perfection.

It sounds so stupid to me now. Naïve for sure. And when none of those things came to fruition, it destroyed me and my relationship with God. It took months and even years in the trenches to learn the things I've shared in this section on Loving.

But even after learning all those things, I still did not understand His sovereignty.

Biblical Examples of Surrendering to God's Sovereignty

Many people in the Bible exemplify surrender to God's sovereignty. I think of Jesus and Job. Jesus wanted to avoid the suffering of the cross. He must have understood the cosmic plan to redeem creation back to God. He was in control and understood. Yet even He asked to avoid the suffering. He wanted something different than the cosmic plan. In Matthew 26:39, we see Jesus praying, "My Father, if it is possible, may this cup be taken from me." He prayed that two more times, even though He knew what the outcome would be. He was surrendered to the sovereignty of God.

In Mark's telling of the same event (Mark 14:6), Jesus uses the word "Abba" when asking to be spared crucifixion. "Abba" in the Aramaic language is a very personal term akin to the English word "Daddy." So, Jesus is begging His daddy to spare Him from a brutal execution. Who of us could deny such a plea from a beloved child? Everyone who loved Jesus, especially his mother, could not understand how this heinous thing could be good or right. Indeed, many people get hung up on this aspect of Christianity. It does not make sense that a good, all-powerful God would need Jesus's death to redeem us back to Him. But God is sovereign, and He knows better. It can be a bitter pill to swallow. Believe me, I know.

And Jesus modeled well for us here. After each plea, He quickly added, "Yet not as I will, but as you will" (Matthew 26:39).

Jesus understood that He must surrender His will to the will of the Father.

Jesus also, being fully man and fully God, experienced the helpless fears of being human and cried out to the Father in desperation. He understood how gut-wrenchingly hard it is to surrender to God's sovereignty, to trust Him in the middle of terrible circumstances that God does not seem interested in thwarting. Thank You, Jesus, for being willing to experience that uniquely human struggle so I can go to You when I am in a similar desperate place, knowing You understand.

And then there's Job. Job was an exceptionally blessed man in every area of life . . . until he was completely stripped of his wealth, family, and health. He was left on the ground covered in oozing sores, poor, destitute, and grieving the loss of all his children. The book chronicles his process of grief and pain. Finally, beginning in chapter 38, the Lord speaks to Job out of a storm. It starts like this:

Who is this that obscures my plans with words without knowledge? Brace
yourself like a man; I will question you, and you shall answer me.
(Job 38:2–3)

The next three chapters are intense as God begins to ask Job things like,

Where were you when I laid the earth's foundation?
(Job 38:4)

Have you ever given orders to the morning, or shown the dawn its place?
(Job 38:12)

Can you bind the chains of the Pleiades? Can you loosen
Orion's belt? Can you bring forth the constellations in
their seasons or lead out the Bear with its cubs?
(Job 38:31–32)

Does the hawk take flight by your wisdom? . . .
Does the eagle soar at your command?
(Job 39:26–27)

The questions are meant to overwhelm Job and cause humility to rise in him as he is faced with the reality of God's goodness, power, and sovereignty.

It works, and Job finally responds:

> I know that you can do all things; no purpose of yours can be thwarted.
> (Job 42:2)
>
> ༄
>
> My ears had heard of you but now my eyes have seen you.
> Therefore I despise myself and repent in dust and ashes.
> (Job 42:5–6)

Job suffered and wrestled with God's sovereignty. I also love how God interacted intensely with Job. The book of Job has a happy ending in that his health and wealth were restored and then some. He had more children and lived a very long life. But God is sovereign, and that may not be the case for everyone.

So the question remains: *Will you surrender?*

My Final Lesson

I thought the skillful and tireless execution of all my good plans should give me control, but the truth was that I had absolutely no control over my children or anything else in the world. I have precious little control of myself, and I'm best to focus there.

Even as I was learning and growing in forgiveness, humility, and faith, I secretly hoped that if I grew enough in those areas, God would give me my heart's desire for my daughter's life and choices. That's so embarrassing to admit. It sounds selfish, controlling, and dumb. If I'm really honest, that was my hope. But God said no, which gave me another opportunity to surrender to Him more.

It's so weird how I can think I'm surrendered, self is dead, I'm at peace, I've released all control—and then something happens, and I'm suddenly aware that I'm not surrendered at all, I have no peace, and I desperately want control. *Ugh!* And then I humble myself again, experience God in power and love, and I'm undone again.

I release control on this journey to freedom, knowing it's an illusion anyway. I work to stay out of denial and live in the reality that I am not the decider of the outcome of my life and definitely not of my children's lives.

When I choose to pursue God rather than any particular outcome on earth, I am free of generational bondage and absolutely everything that ties me down or attempts to deceive me.

> True love and freedom come when I surrender to God's sovereignty.

I wish I could convince you to yield your will to Jesus. How can I persuade you to live out "Thy will be done"? So often, we think our will is aligned with God's will, and just as often, we are mistaken. We don't see the picture clearly.

In 1 Corinthians 13:12, Paul said, "For now we see only a reflection as in a mirror; then we shall see face to face. Now I know in part; then I shall know fully, even as I am fully known." Ah, how I long for that day.

We think we're in the know. We think we know better. We have all the details of the problems in our lives, our friends' lives, and our children's lives. We know right from wrong. We understand which habits lead to certain futures. We may even know what the Bible says. So we think we know what God wants. We draw lines from the Bible to the lives of our children, friends, and family, and we think we know exactly what needs to happen for us and others to walk out God's will.

But another crazy paradox is that God gives us life experiences, reasoning minds, His Law written on our hearts (our conscience), and His Holy Word to show us His will, yet somehow we cannot manage to walk in His will, even using those obvious tools. That's because we're trying on our own. We can only walk in His will by forsaking everything of our own will, which is a culmination of all the things listed above. Even as I began to walk in powerful aspects of God's will, such as forgiveness, repentance, humility, death to self, faith, and, above all, Love, I still did not understand His will. Honestly, I still don't understand it because I see only in part. And honestly, I'm so concerned with my little life that I can't see His galactic plan.

So I'll say it clearly. This is the final surrender. God is sovereign. He decides. My flesh does not like that.

When God allowed Amanda to marry Steven, I was dumbfounded. I thought I had surrendered my will the night before their wedding, and I did in the spirit. But once the day was over and I had that terrible nightmare/vision, I was walking in my flesh alone again. I could not wrap my head around the plan. I could only see bad coming out of this. My husband wouldn't allow Steven into our home at that point. Therefore, my daughter was pulled and knew that she needed to choose her husband ultimately, although she was trying to mend things and coming to family gatherings without Steven if she could.

The whole thing was awkward and sad. So much was unsaid. There was so much brokenness all around. They were living in that shack, and we would hear of the spotty electrical issues there, especially when it rained, which made us concerned about a fire hazard. On stormy nights, we fell asleep with visions of the place catching fire and killing our daughter. She told us of waking up with ants crawling all over her and biting her on summer nights. The list goes on and on. I had to keep reminding myself that she lived in America, less than three miles from our home, where the weather was mild, she had food and water, and I could get to her easily within seven minutes in case of emergency. (I timed it.)

I had to keep telling myself this because, to my standards, she was living in unacceptable conditions. How could this be a part of God's will? There was such a better way. In fact, we had laid out the plan for the better way. I mean, clearly, she and Steven were outside of God's will. So, why had God allowed this marriage to happen when I was on my face on the floor, crying out to Him—imploring, begging, standing on His promises? This was God's will? What?

Surrendering to His sovereignty was my final lesson. Too often, it does not seem that God is in control. We only have to look around our immediate circles to see lives full of regret and pain and ugliness. And then, if we turn on the news or take a deep dive into the goings-on around the world, it looks like a sinister evil being is executing a malevolent plan. How can God be in control? How could so much bad exist with a sovereign, good God?

Final Surrender

Looking at my situation, it seemed like God had decided that He wanted to be the only Lord before me, regardless of my pleas. It felt like God let me down, and He wanted me to *forgive* Him (as well as everyone else). It felt like He knew better, no matter how bad it looked to me, and my *faith* needed to increase. It felt like He wanted me to accept His final word even when I disagreed entirely with every fiber of my being. I needed *death to self*—an even more complete death than ever before. It felt like humiliation and a mockery of my life, and He wanted to *humble* me more. It felt like He didn't love me, and He wanted me to *Love Him* even when I felt forsaken. He wanted me to *Love others* even when they betrayed me. And I could not do any of this without unabashedly *pursuing intimacy* with Holy Spirit.

Every lesson I needed to learn was tied together and wrapped up in this idea of God's sovereignty. He is sovereign. It's not a cop-out to not be able to explain the problem of pain and suffering. Other people have worked more earnestly on that topic. Many books have been written because it is such a sticking point of faith for so many. For me, I just sat on my living room floor and said, "Why?" over and over. "I don't understand, God. Why?"

He wanted me to be alone with Him, and He responded, "Because I said so . . . you will understand later . . . you only see in part . . . it's the wrong prayer."

So I took a deep breath. I asked Holy Spirit to give me the right prayer. I listened. I kept breathing. A tear ran down my cheek as I prayed, "I praise You for Your sovereignty. You are great. You are the only wise and righteous One. I am not right. Let Your Kingdom come. Let Your will be done. Let me help to bring it on earth as it is in heaven."

And He said, "*Yes.*"

Reflections on Loving

Thank you for endeavoring through this book with me. I am truly honored. I hope I have given you a taste of freedom and how to get it. I invite you to begin your journey with the end in mind. Allow Holy Spirit to guide you as you reflect on the following questions.

1. What painful generational patterns do you want to break free from?

_____

_____

_____

_____

_____

_____

_____

_____

2. After reading this book, how do you think your life would be different if you had freedom?

_____

_____

_____

_____

_____

_____

_____

_____

_____

_____

_____

_____

_____

_____

_____

3. How would you be different?

_____

_____

_____

_____

_____

_____

_____

_____

_____

_____

_____

_____

_____

This is a photo taken the week I first met Barbara. She was nineteen, and I was twenty. We had gone camping at Kern River. You can see Jeff's 1967 Bronco. We still have that thing!

This photo was taken of Barb and me a few years ago when we hosted a prayer retreat at our cabin in Shaver Lake, California. It was a glorious weekend.

Hank (5)

Levi (2)

Franklin and me (2023)

Amanda, Steven, and Franklin at their wedding (2016)

This is my mom and me in 2019. We had just finished watching the musical "Wicked" in Hollywood. Thirty minutes after this photo was taken, I was verbally assaulted by the man that ended up crying and hugging me and confessing to me in the middle of Hollywood Blvd.

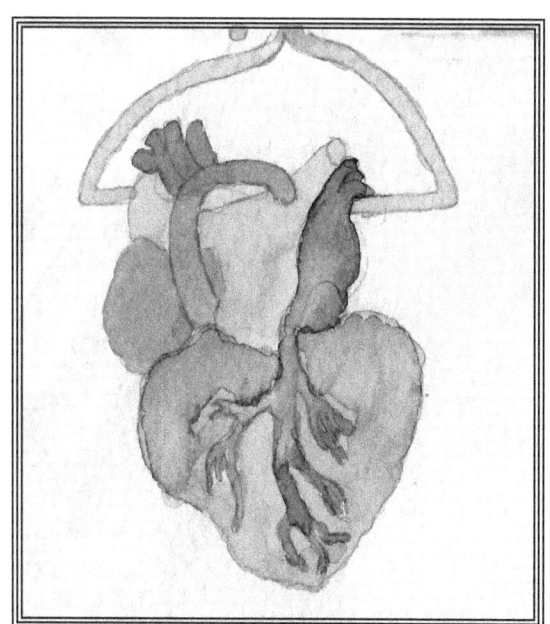

One of my clients painted this heart hanging on a hanger after hearing about my dream about the walk-in closet. Pretty cool reminder to gather hearts rather than shoes.

NOTES

Introduction

1   American Academy of Child & Adolescent Psychiatry, "Alcohol Use in Families," no. 17; updated May 2017, https://www.aacap.org/AACAP/Families_and_Youth/Facts_for_Families/FFF-Guide/Children-Of-Alcoholics-017.aspx.

2   Office for National Statistics, "People who were abused as children are more likely to be abused as an adult: Exploring the impact of what can sometimes be hidden crimes," https://www.ons.gov.uk/peoplepopulationandcommunity/crimeandjustice/articles/peoplewhowereabusedaschildrenaremorelikelytobeabusedasanadult/2017-09-27.

Chapter 1

3   "Merriam-Webster, s.v. "codependency," accessed August 16, 2022, https://www.merriam-webster.com/dictionary/codependency.

4   Beattie, Melody, *Codependent No More: How to Stop Controlling Others and Start Caring for Yourself* (Center City, MN: Hazelden Publishing, 1992), 35.

Chapter 5

5   Gilbert, Roberta M., *The Eight Concepts of Bowen Theory* (Lake Frederick, VA: Leading Systems Press, 2005), 12.

6   Gilbert, *The Eight Concepts of Bowen Theory,* 5.

7   Gilbert, *The Eight Concepts of Bowen Theory,* 29.

8   Gilbert, *The Eight Concepts of Bowen Theory*, 49.

9   Gilbert, *The Eight Concepts of Bowen Theory*, 25.

10   "Multigenerational Transmission Process," The Bowen Center for the Study of the Family, accessed August 20, 2022, https://www.thebowencenter.org/multigenerational-transmission-process.

11   Walker, Lenore E., "Cycle of Abuse theory to explain patterns of behavior in an abusive relationship," 1979, Wikipedia, https://en.wikipedia.org/wiki/Cycle_of_abuse.

Chapter 7

12   Malone, Henry, *Shadow Boxing: The Dynamic 2-5-14 Strategy to Defeat the Darkness Within* (Lewisville, TX: Vision Life Publications, 2011), 87.

Chapter 8

13   Lemmel, Helen H., "Turn Your Eyes upon Jesus." Public domain.

Chapter 12

14   Referring to Amanda's learning disabilities, sibling rivalries, my frustration tolerance, juggling schedules, etc.

15   Dronen, Christina, 2020. "True Meaning of Repentance—It's Better Than You Think." Gentlechristianparenting. March 15, 2020. https://gentlechristianparenting.com/repentance-meaning/.

16   Dronen, "True Meaning of Repentance—It's Better Than You Think."

Chapter 13

17   Baker, Heidi, *Birthing the Miraculous* (Lake Mary, Florida: Charisma House, 2014), 20.

18   Shir, Pinchas, "Who Were the Two Thieves?" Israel Bible Weekly, May 18, 2022, https://weekly.israelbiblecenter.com/who-were-the-two-thieves/.

Chapter 14

19   Garden Apostolic Training Center School of Ministry, "Kingdom I Manual," compiled and edited by Brandy Helton (Sterling City, Texas: Garden Publishing Company, 2008).

Chapter 17

20 Fénelon, François, *Let Go to Get Peace and Real Joy* (New Kensington, PA: Whitaker House, 1973), 15.

21 Sarah was a client of mine that I tried to help recover from anorexia for about twelve years, and during this time, she died from anorexia nervosa. Her name has been changed to protect confidentiality.

22 Jasmine is Franklin's mother.

Chapter 18

23 Fénelon, François, *Let Go to Get Peace and Real Joy* (New Kensington, PA: Whitaker House, 1973), 11.

Chapter 19

24 "Paradox," Lexico.com, https://www.lexico.com/en/definition/paradox.

25 Grudem, Wayne, *Systematic Theology: An Introduction to Biblical Doctrine* (Grand Rapids: Zondervan, 1994), 217.

ABOUT THE AUTHOR

*A*uthor and speaker Rena Roberts splits her time between Southern California and South Dakota. She loves the mountains and the sea and enjoys hiking, water skiing, and spending hours on the beach connecting deeply with those most cherished. She loves to cook and share her home with friends and family, often one and the same as far as she is concerned.

As a licensed marriage and family therapist, Rena has specialized in treating eating disorders for over twenty years. She was a primary therapist at Monte Nido Residential Treatment Center, the clinical director at the Eating Disorder Center of California, and ran an intensive outpatient program at Charter Hospital in Thousand Oaks, CA, under Carolyn Costin.

Now, Rena loves to counsel and pray with whomever God sends her way...women at church, couples she's known for years, homeless people in front of her local drug store, her children and their friends, and her husband's customers. Her highest hope is to bring the Love and Light of God everywhere she goes.

Long Live Love is Rena's first writing endeavor, a book born out of a life of overcoming and surrendering. People who know Rena's story have often told her she should write a book. But the time and inclination were not right for her until now. To connect with Rena or have her speak for your next church event or retreat, connect with her at RenaRoberts.com or email her at Rena@RenaRoberts.com.

Rena and her husband, Jeff, have been married for thirty-two years. They have three grown children and three grandsons who bring them great joy and laughter. They are grateful.

♡